○ Walking Eye

KU-227-648

**Discover the world's best d[...]
app, available to download for free in the App [...]**

The container app provides easy access to fantastic free content on events and activities taking place in your current location or chosen destination, with the possibility of booking, as well as the regularly-updated Insight Guides travel blog: Inspire Me. In addition, you can purchase curated, premium destination guides through the app, which feature local highlights, hotel, bar, restaurant and shopping listings, an A to Z of practical information and more. Or purchase and download Insight Guides eBooks straight to your device.

INSIGHT ○ GUIDES

Walking Eye

○ DESTINATIONS

⊘ INSPIRE ME

🗐 EBOOKS

🗓 EVENTS

TOP 10 ATTRACTIONS

THE GETTY CENTER
The museum has a great Western art collection. See page 44.

VENICE BEACH
There's always something going on here. See page 50.

DOWNTOWN LA
Historic streets and impressive landmark buildings. See page 53.

RODEO DRIVE
Shop alongside the rich and famous. See page 40.

INTRODUCTION

Los Angeles, perhaps more than any other place on earth, is preceded by its reputation. Here is a city teeming with movie stars, exorbitant wealth, sunny beaches, palm trees, and beautiful people. But LA is also linked with adventure and maybe even danger, complete with earthquakes, floods, crime, and scandals of global proportions. Because the world is watching, it's a town eternally destined to make a spectacle of itself, whether on-screen or in real life. The result is a modern-day 'Wild West' meshed with everyday life, where image is reality, poverty clashes with wealth, and fame is acquired overnight – all publicized to the hilt around the globe.

The world's perception, however, hardly reflects the real Los Angeles. The city is not merely beautiful coastlines, hit TV shows, opulent mansions in the hills, and the latest in celebrity gossip. Los Angeles County is a collection of 88 separate cities packed between the Pacific Ocean and Orange and San Bernardino counties. Many of these towns have their own city halls, police forces, and fire brigades. The result is that LA is a place without a geographic heart, but with lots of soul. If its soul is superficial, flighty, and playful – well, this is the entertainment capital of the world.

A VARIETY OF LIFESTYLES

Los Angeles encompasses a huge variety of American life within its borders. In fact, the cultural and economic lifestyles of some 10 million county residents vary so enormously from area to area that visiting Los Angeles is like visiting half a dozen destinations at once. You can go casual and carefree with the beach scene, blow the bank on a ritzy Beverly Hills shopping excursion, retreat to nature on a mountain hike, opt for the 'global' by touring the ethnic neighborhoods, flee to fantasy at any number of amusement parks, or simply entertain yourself with an exploration into the entertainment world and Hollywood exotica. Whatever you do, you'll experience in-your-face LA, because its eccentricities are abundant wherever you go.

The one attribute that suffuses everything in Los Angeles is its lively energy. Even on your first visit there's no denying the feeling that something – somewhere – is about to happen. It might be catching the eye of your favorite celebrity scurrying into a movie theater, watching a production company shoot a scene from the next big

Downtown LA

blockbuster movie, attempting to keep up with the freeway's pedal-to-the-metal drivers, or simply scanning the twinkling evening skyline from the heights of the Griffith Observatory. In a town where the fast lane is the norm and Hollywood isn't just a place but a state of being, you can't help feeling part of something exciting and unpredictable.

LARGE ETHNIC POPULATIONS

Much of this energy can be attributed to the residents. Few places on earth attract such a diverse population. The year-round sunshine appeals to all kinds and LA offers an ideal combination of urban and beach living. Add to this the enter-tainment industry folk and then LA's large groups of Americans of Chinese, African, Korean, Middle Eastern, and Japanese

The freeway

descent. Hispanic Americans comprise the largest ethnic group of all, numbering around 49 percent of the population.

With so many people packed into such a condensed area, Angelenos are constantly struggling to create unique identities for themselves, which would be more of a challenge if the town didn't have such an 'anything goes' attitude.

CITY OF FREEWAYS

What comes as no surprise is that the car is king. With nearly two vehicles per household, LA has one of the world's highest per-capita car populations. Visitors will have to join the masses traveling the streets and freeways to get a real feel for the city.

Tourist attractions are scattered from Malibu all the way to Disneyland but much of what you'll see will be through your car window because you'll likely be spending a lot of time driving. Used by over 12 million vehicles daily, the nation's 10 busiest freeways are all in the LA vicinity. Strict emission controls have considerably reduced the city's notorious smog, but air quality can still be poor. To combat highway congestion and pollution, LA is expanding its much-needed light rail network. The good news, however, is that freeway exits and visitor attractions are well marked, and you're bound to find an unexpected attraction to get you off the road and back to the excitement in no time.

A BRIEF HISTORY

Long before the arrival of Spanish colonists, this part of the West Coast was a pastoral home to 30,000 Native American Indians. In 1542, Juan Rodriguez Cabrillo, a Portuguese navigator in the service of Carlos I, king of Spain, was the first European to set foot in the area. But for the next two centuries LA remained nothing more than a pit stop on the trans-Pacific naval highway – a provisioning spot for Spanish galleons on their way back to Mexico from the Philippines. It wasn't until other nations cast their eyes towards California that Spain decided to strengthen its claim on the region through colonization.

FOUNDING COLONISTS

In 1769, Spanish colonists, led by two men, a 55-year-old Franciscan priest named Father Junípero Serra and Captain Gaspar de Portolá, arrived in San Diego and built the first of a string of missions up the coast to consolidate territories, extend borders, and bring Christianity to Native Americans. Natives didn't take well to the new lifestyle, and diseases that arrived with the colonists killed so many thousands that the Native American population of California never recovered from the initial encounter.

In 1771, Mission San Gabriel Arcangel was founded, marking the first major Spanish presence in the Los Angeles area. It was the fourth in the mission chain and still stands 9 miles (14.5km) east of LA. Within the next few years California's military governor Felipe de Neve decided the area needed a settlement and made plans to design a *pueblo*, or town. It took months to recruit any settlers, but in 1781, a group of 12 men, 11 women, and 21 children arrived at the mission from Mexico, and on September 4 they ceremoniously founded the new town 'El Pueblo de Nuestra Señora la Reina de Los Angeles de

Porciúncula' (Our Lady the Queen of the Angels of Porciúncula).
Today the site is better known as Downtown's Olvera Street.

Prosperity came slowly. In 1800, the population was 315.
The *pueblo* included 30 homes, a town hall and guardhouse,
granaries, a church, a central plaza, and 12,500 cows.

THE CALIFORNIA RANCHOS

De Neve's successor passed new laws enabling him to grant
vast tracts of land and grazing rights to settlers. He distrib-
uted tens of thousands of acres, largely to his friends and
comrades. It was not long before a dozen or so *patrones*
(landlords) owned nearly all of what is now coastal Los
Angeles County, with the exception of the mission lands and
the farms surrounding the *pueblo*.

Because colonial powers controlled all trade in their territories, Mexico and Spain at first received the wealth of goods

The Great Wall of Los Angeles

produced by the California *ranchos* (ranches or farms) and missions. But news soon made its way to the East Coast about cheap goods from the California settlements. With few Spanish ships or militia in the area to enforce colonial trading laws, Yankee ships began capitalizing on this lucrative market, ending California's isolation.

MEXICAN RULE AND AMERICAN ANNEXATION

After Mexico declared independence from Spain in 1822 and claimed California for itself in 1825, Spanish priests were ordered out of the region and missions lost their power. Commissioners were appointed to distribute 8 million acres (3 million hectares) of mission land and resources, most to powerful families and ranchers. The Native Americans, having lost their lands, either fled to the mountains or found themselves having to work for Mexican landlords.

Meanwhile, the *pueblo* of Los Angeles had become the largest settlement in the territory, with a population of nearly 1,250. A number of Americans had settled in California, joined the Catholic Church, and married into the area's leading families. Within a few years, these Americans became great landholders and wielded a monopoly on local commerce.

By the time war erupted between the United States and Mexico in 1846, agitators in Washington were already calling for the annexation of California. The Mexican settlers put up a good fight, against forces several times their number. Eventually, they were defeated, and in January 1847, General Andrés Pico relinquished Los Angeles to the Americans.

AFTER THE GOLD RUSH

Growth was still slow, but the discovery of gold in northern California in 1848 changed everything. Many Angelenos packed their bags and headed out to dig; those who stayed

Miners in the 1850s Gold Rush

found a lucrative market in supplying food and goods to miners. Meat replaced hides and tallow as the main industry of the ranches; cattle were herded north where they could be sold for ten times the going rate.

On April 4, 1850, the city of Los Angeles was incorporated and declared the county seat. Its first newspaper, *The Star*, began in the same year, published in both Spanish and English. Over the next 20 years, Los Angeles gained a reputation as a 'bad' town, with the largest number of gambling dens, brothels, and saloons per capita in the West. But new industries sprang up: wine became an important export; the first citrus trees were planted; and a water-supply system was installed. Los Angeles began to lose its frontier-town aspects.

THE BOOM YEARS

By 1870, Los Angeles' population numbered 5,614. Hotels and larger buildings were constructed; civic and cultural institutions such as a library, a dance academy, and a drama society were founded. Further prosperity followed the completion of the Southern Pacific Railroad line to Los Angeles in 1876, making the vital transcontinental link and sparking the biggest real-estate boom in the nation's history.

As the large *ranchos* were gradually divided, settlers planted orchards and gardens and introduced modern agricultural methods. Oranges became one of the major crops, when refrigerated rail cars arrived.

In late 1885, the Santa Fe Railroad line reached Los Angeles, competing with the Southern Pacific in a fierce price war that made cross-country travel virtually free. By 1887, trains had brought more than 120,000 to the town of 10,000 residents; most of the travelers settled in the area.

The real-estate boom collapsed three years after it began, but by the time the dust settled in 1890, Los Angeles had embarked on a new campaign designed to lure Midwestern farmers to the sunny state. California's prize agricultural produce was vigorously promoted, and people poured into the area believing the motto the city still promotes: 'LA is the place where fortunes are made and dreams come true.'

The discovery of petroleum in 1892, not far from the city center, prompted another flurry of development and added a few more names to the growing list of ultra-wealthy residents. The first well, drilled by Edward Doheny and Charles Canfield, yielded 45 barrels a day. Within five years nearly 2,500 wells had been sunk within the city limits, and the industry flourished. Led by Los Angeles, California produced a quarter

Small beginnings

With the rapidly expanding population, Los Angeles city lots were bought up quickly and new communities were founded. One of these, created by Horace and Daeida Wilcox when they subdivided their 120-acre (48-hectare) orchard, was named 'Hollywood.'

William Mulholland – the man who built the city's water infrastructure

of the world's oil supply right into the 20th century.

The 1890s marked further expansion with the construction of San Pedro's deep-water harbor. Port of Los Angeles, the largest man-made port in the world, opened in 1910.

THE 20TH CENTURY

During its first 120 years, Los Angeles had become a dynamic city with a population of more than 100,000. But with a new advertising venture that included the slogan 'Oranges for Health – California for Wealth,' the population of the city tripled in the first decade of the 20th century.

One concern stood in the way of further expansion: water – or, rather, the lack of it. As the population mushroomed, it became clear that the Los Angeles River, the sole source of water for the city, would not be able to support the city's needs. William Mulholland, chief engineer of the Municipal Water Bureau, planned to obtain water from the Owens River, which was fed by snow-melt from the High Sierra. In an amazing feat of determination, an aqueduct more than 233 miles (375km) long was constructed to deliver enough water to supply a city of 2 million. As an added benefit, a hydroelectric generating plant was completed along the aqueduct in 1917. In 1923, with the population rising by 100,000 each year, it was clear that an additional supply of water would soon be needed. Mulholland began to survey a route for a waterway from the Colorado River, 400 miles (644km) away in Arizona. The new aqueducts opened in 1939.

After World War I, LA became the fastest-growing city in the United States. The metropolis soon stretched from the southern harbor at San Pedro to the San Fernando Valley in the north. A streetcar system began operating in 1901, and by the late 1930s had become the largest in the US, servicing some 80 million passengers a year. Citrus crops accounted for a third of the county's produce. It was the nation's richest agricultural region. Large oil refineries were built, and with the coming of Firestone and Goodyear, LA also became a major rubber-producing center, which seems especially appropriate, considering its residents' already-established love affair with the car. Later, aircraft and car assembly plants were built. No single business, however, was – or is – as enduring in Los Angeles as the motion picture industry, which in 1919 was already making 80 percent of the world's supply of films. It has remained the city's chief industry.

In the 1920s Los Angeles was a boom town and a melting pot for immigrants, hustlers, adventurers, desperados, and dreamers. Institutions appropriate for a burgeoning city were built, including Downtown's historic Biltmore Hotel, the Central Library, City Hall, and the University of Southern California (which was founded in 1880).

Mulholland's drive

In 1924, LA honored water engineer William Mulholland by naming scenic Mulholland Drive after him. His work had given the city a reliable water supply. But 1928 brought disaster. A dam 40 miles (25km) north of Los Angeles collapsed only hours after he had inspected it, killing 450 people. Mulholland resigned in disgrace.

Hollywood Walk of Fame

When the Great Depression struck in 1929, southern California's growth slowed as dispossessed farmers of the Dust Bowl region (the south-central United States) and a long line of other not-so-welcome migrants headed west. But by 1935 the city was optimistic, recovering economically, and ranking fifth among the industrial counties of the US.

World War II brought further growth in industry and population, as workers flocked to LA to find jobs at aircraft plants and shipyards. Close to 200,000 African Americans moved into south-central LA to pursue job opportunities. Mexican residents, who had not been so welcome after the end of Mexican rule, were also accepted as laborers. But overcrowding, prejudice, and already obvious social ranking would continue to cause great tensions.

With the postwar population boom and the phaseout of LA's streetcars came the mass construction of today's freeway system, making possible the development of areas previously considered too remote. Along one of these freeway routes in Orange County was another major construction project, Disneyland, which was surrounded by orange groves when it opened in 1955.

THE WATTS RIOTS

By 1963, California had become America's most populous state. More water shortages, reduced services, and increased racial tensions resulted. In the summer of 1965, widespread rioting broke out in the black ghetto of Watts, in south-central LA, when a black motorist was accused of drink-driving. Six days of vandalism, looting, and fires left 34 dead and caused $40 million in damage. The scene was repeated in the spring of 1992, when the acquittal of four white policemen accused of beating black motorist Rodney King sparked 48 hours of riotous violence. The death toll reached 50, with thousands injured and property damage of over $1 billion. While other trials (O.J. Simpson's murder trial in 1995, for example) divided the city, others, including recovery from the 1994 Northridge earthquake, brought Angelenos together as a community. A strengthening economy in Southern California has helped as well.

FILMED IN HOLLYWOOD

Movies found a home in southern California because the sunny days and wide-open spaces were perfect for filmmaking. Cecil B. DeMille set up the town's first movie studio near Highland and Sunset in a horse barn and filmed *The Squaw Man*, the first feature-length film, in 1913. In the 1920s a box-office boom, led by such Hollywood stars as Douglas Fairbanks, Charlie Chaplin, and Mary Pickford, made movies a lucrative business. By 1939 cinemas out-numbered banks, and Americans spent twice as much time at the movies as they do today.

In the latter part of the 20th century, the Hollywood area's golden history was tarnished by decay as the studios and stars moved out and an ongoing parade of hustlers and lost souls, souvenir shops and touristy attractions moved in. But since the millennium, an extensive renovation program has brought shiny new attractions and entertainment venues that will ensure the city's encore performance.

City of Los Angeles Police

By the 1980s the growth of the metropolitan region forced city planners to begin rebuilding a system of public transport. A new light rail line, the Metro Blue Line, opened in 1990, connecting Downtown to Long Beach. The Red Line, the first subway, opened Downtown in 1993, and now stretches all the way to North Hollywood. The Green and Gold light rail lines, opened in 1995 and 2003 respectively, were joined in 2005 by the Orange Line, a dedicated bus transitway through the San Fernando Valley, and in 2006 by the Purple Line subway, serving west of Downtown. The latest addition is an extension to the Expo Line to the west with seven new stations linking Santa Monica with Downtown in under 50 minutes.

LA FOREVER

Los Angeles' sprawl has made creating a unified 'city' impossible. Though the entertainment industry and its revenues reach businesses and residents from Downtown to Malibu, in almost every other way each neighborhood is its own mini-city struggling for a sense of itself. Los Angeles County with a population of over 10 million is facing the challenges of the 21st century as well as the perennial problems of soaring prices for energy and basic necessities. But that doesn't prevent Angelenos from looking on the bright side. Business is booming; the beach is packed; and movie stars and millionaires are still made overnight.

HISTORICAL LANDMARKS

1771 Founding of Mission San Gabriel Arcangel.

1781 Founding of El Pueblo de Nuestra Señora la Reina de Los Angeles de Porciúncula.

1825 California becomes a territory of Mexico.

1848 The treaty of Guadalupe Hidalgo ends the Mexican-American War. California annexed to the US, becoming a state in 1850.

1853 Don Matteo Keeler plants the first orange trees.

1876 First transcontinental railroad, the Southern Pacific, arrives.

1880 The University of Southern California is founded.

1881 The *Los Angeles Times* publishes its first issue.

1892 Oil is discovered in downtown Los Angeles.

1913 Cecil B. DeMille makes the first full-length feature film, *The Squaw Man*, in a barn near Highland and Sunset.

1923 The Hollywood sign is erected.

1927 Grauman's Chinese Theatre opens. The Academy of Motion Picture Arts and Sciences is founded at the Biltmore Hotel.

1928 LA's first airport, Mines Field, opens.

1932 The Summer Olympics take place in LA.

1947 Hollywood Freeway links Downtown with the Valley.

1955 Disneyland opens in Anaheim.

1961 The Hollywood Walk of Fame is launched.

1965 The Watts riots.

1984 The XXIII Olympiad is held in LA.

1992 Riots in reaction to the verdict in the Rodney King trial.

1993 LA's first subway line, the Red Line, opens in Downtown.

1994 The Northridge earthquake causes much destruction.

1995 The O.J. Simpson trial captures the world's attention.

2003 The Walt Disney Concert Hall opens at the Music Center.

2006 Getty Villa reopens in Malibu after a major restoration.

2011 'Carmageddon' strands Angelenos when the 405 freeway is shut down for two days.

2012 The Expo Line between Downtown and Culver City starts.

2015 The Broad, a new landmark contemporary art museum, opens.

WHERE TO GO

To savor the abundant flavors of LA, you need a taste for adventure, a car (ideally), and a good map. Add savvy plans that keep you off the freeways during rush hour, and you will discover why Angelenos consider their home the center of the universe. Visit Hollywood by day for its remnants of old-time movie-world glamour, or after dark for its theaters and nightclubs. Star-gazing in Beverly Hills or a night out on the Sunset Strip are also favorite LA experiences. For culture, head for the Wilshire District's Museum Row, the Westside's Getty Center and Hammer Museum, or Pasadena's superb art museums. Downtown has some of the city's finest architecture, historic sites, and vibrant neighbourhoods offering a mix of ethnicities. And no trip to LA is complete without at least one day on the beach and a visit to the Santa Monica pier. The surrounding mountains and valleys, along with Orange County to the south, offer theme parks, historic missions and wildlife reserves. For a longer excursion, you can escape to Palm Springs or Catalina Island.

HOLLYWOOD

'Hollywood' is not merely an actual place but, rather, a lifestyle unique to Los Angeles. While the city of Hollywood might once have had a glamorous reputation, during the past few decades the neighborhood, which stretches along

Tourist information

The city's main visitor information centers are located at the Hollywood & Highland Center and downtown at 685 South Figueroa Street, but many areas of the metro region also have their own tourist offices (see page 131).

Rooftop Bar at the Standard Hotel, Downtown

The iconic Hollywood sign

the base of the northern hills emblazoned with the land-mark Hollywood sign, deteriorated like a faded movie star. Now, it has been making a major comeback as one of the city's trendiest spots for shopping, dining, and night-time entertainment.

TINSELTOWN TRIUMPHS

The **Hollywood sign** over Beachwood Canyon is perhaps the most recognized landmark in LA and a favorite photo background. Originally constructed in 1923 to promote real-estate sales in the neighborhood then called 'Hollywoodland,' the 50ft (15m) letters were abbreviated in later years and replaced due to age in 1978. Even though you can't get close enough to the sign to touch it (it has a security system sur-rounding it, but a challenging hike via Griffith Park will bring you pretty close), it's still a powerful and beloved symbol, reminding visitors of Los Angeles' status as the center of the fast and glamorous world of movie making.

Equally famous is the **Hollywood Walk of Fame ❶**. The 'walk' refers to the legwork you'll need to do to check out the 2,300 or so bronze-and-terrazzo stars embedded in the pavement to honor celebrities in the music and entertainment industries. Stars stretch for a total of 3.5 miles (5.5km) along Hollywood Boulevard from La Brea Avenue to Gower Street, and along Vine Street from Yucca Street to Sunset Boulevard. Among the most sought-after are those of Marilyn Monroe (in front of McDonald's at 6774 Hollywood Boulevard), Charlie Chaplin (at 6751), and John Wayne (1541 Vine). To find the location of your favorite, visit www.walkoffame.com/star finder. What does it take to get one's name on a star? You must be nominated to the Hollywood Chamber of Commerce and, if selected, come up with $25,000 to pay for your star.

TCL Chinese Theatre ❷, still often referred to as Grauman's Chinese Theatre (6925 Hollywood Boulevard; tel: 323-463 9576 for tours; www.tclchinesetheatres.com), which you can't miss due to its flashy Chinese temple-style architecture and the swarms of tourists out front, is one of the other worthwhile stops on Hollywood Boulevard. While current films are still shown here, the real attraction is the exterior courtyard, where autographs, handprints and footprints in cement commemorate Hollywood's greatest celebrities. This Art-Deco picture palace, originally called The Grauman, was built by the great showman Sid Grauman in 1927. The courtyard tradition allegedly began at the opening, when actress Norma Talmadge accidentally stepped in wet cement. Among the famous signatures, you can also spot such unusual impressions as Jimmy Durante's nose and the hoof prints of Gene Autry's horse, Champion.

Adjacent to the TCL is the glamorous **Hollywood & Highland** shopping and entertainment complex (http://hollywoodandhighland.com; Mon–Sat 10am–10pm and Sun 10am–7pm), focal point of the city's renovation. It includes the

TCL Chinese Theatre at night

gorgeous Dolby Theatre (formerly known as the Kodak Theatre), permanent home of the Academy Awards; the Loews Hollywood Hotel; and Babylon Court, modeled after the set from the 1916 film *Intolerance*, with a grand staircase, 33ft (10m) pillars topped by a pair of elephants, and an archway that frames the Hollywood sign in the background. The Visitor Information Center (Mon–Sat 9am–10pm, Sun 10am–7pm) is the place to pick up half-price theater tickets to shows playing throughout the city. Tickets become available on Tuesdays for productions running that week, so you can book ahead as well as attend same-day shows.

While Grauman's is undoubtedly the hotspot for your 'That's-me-in-Hollywood!' snapshots, the area's other landmark cinemas deserve a peek as well. *Citizen Kane* premiered in 1941 at the Moorish-style **El Capitan Theatre** (6838 Hollywood Boulevard; https://elcapitantheatre.com), which today is a primary venue for Disney films. **The Egyptian Theatre** (6712 Hollywood Boulevard; tel: 323-466 3456; www.egyptiantheatre.com) was Hollywood's first movie palace, built by Grauman in 1922 after the discovery of Tutankhamen's tomb. Restored in 1998, it shows classic and independent films and has backstage tours once a month. Also noteworthy is the **Hollywood Roosevelt Hotel** (7000 Hollywood Boulevard;

tel: 323-856 1970; www.thehollywoodroosevelt.com), which established itself as the hotel of the film world when it opened in 1927. Just two years later, in 1929, the landmark building hosted the first public Oscar ceremony; it was also home to Marilyn Monroe for eight years. Its lobby features hand-painted ceilings and Spanish-revival décor of wrought-iron grillwork. On display on the mezzanine floor are historic Hollywood photographs and other memorabilia.

The former Max Factor Building, an Art-Deco gem, houses the **Hollywood Museum** (1660 N. Highland Avenue; tel: 323-464 7776; www.thehollywoodmuseum.com; Wed–Sun 10am–5pm). It contains some 5,000 artifacts of movie memorabilia, including costumes, props, posters, and photographs. Hollywood glamour is highlighted in the Max Factor exhibit of movie stars' dressing rooms and make-up cases.

STRICTLY TOURIST

Clustered together on Hollywood Boulevard is a range of cheesy but mildly entertaining attractions that are aimed

OSCARS

A gold-plated bronze figure standing on a reel of film holds a sword upright: this prestigious statuette has been awarded since 1928 for what the Academy of Motion Picture Arts and Sciences judge the year's best achievements in film, for everybody from actors and directors to scriptwriters, costume designers, and technical and effects artists. Why the name Oscar? Until 1931 the statuette had no name, until an obscure Academy librarian, Margaret Herrick (who eventually became its executive director), gave it the nickname because of its resemblance to her Uncle Oscar. The nickname stuck after it was reported in an article in a local newspaper.

squarely at relieving you of your tourist dollars**. Ripley's Believe It or Not!** offers lightweight entertainment, starting with the Tyrannosaurus rex towering above the entrance (6780 Hollywood Boulevard; tel: 323-466 6335; www.ripleys.com/hollywood; daily 10am–midnight). Robert Ripley was a cartoonist who traveled the far corners of the globe in the 1930s and 1940s, searching for examples of the bizarre. His first 'Odditorium' opened at the Chicago World's Fair in 1933, and the cartoon features based on his collection are still syndicated worldwide. Here you'll see a shrunken head, a two-headed goat, and a statue of Marilyn Monroe made of shredded money, among other curiosities.

Capitol Records Tower Building

Next door is the **Guinness World Records Museum** (6764 Hollywood Boulevard; tel: 323-463 6433; www.guinnessmuseumhollywood.com; daily 10am–midnight), which offers two floors of displays about bizarre facts, feats, and achievements. Across the street is the unimpressive **Hollywood Wax Museum** (6767 Hollywood Boulevard; tel: 323-462 5991; www.hollywoodwaxmuseum.com; daily 10am–midnight), featuring a collection of superstars from Jesus Christ to Sylvester Stallone.

Further along you'll spot the flashy pink exterior of **Frederick's of Hollywood**

(6751 Hollywood Boulevard), the shop best known for glamorizing trashy undergarments. Among the racks of feathery satin bras and panties are gallery presentations from their 'Lingerie Museum,' where you can peek at the apparel of celebrities such as Monroe and Madonna.

The intersection of Hollywood and Vine was once the heart of Tinseltown, but now it is rather nondescript, at least by day. A number of nearby

Hollywood Trolley

The Hollywood Trolley are three bus lines operating between Hollywood Beach and the Historic Downtown. One ride costs $1 per person, paid on-board. Trolleys depart approximately every 30 minutes every Wednesday, Thursday and Sunday 10am–10pm and every Friday and Saturday 10am–11pm. For further information and a route map, visit the website: www.visit hollywoodfl.org/trolley.aspx.

theaters make it a busy spot for nightlife. A touch of the old glamour survives in the landmark **Capitol Records Building** ❸ (1750 N. Vine Street), which is shaped like a stack of records. The building's distinctive design is credited to recording stars Nat King Cole and Johnny Mercer. The Hollywood Jazz mural by Richard Wyatt on the south wall depicts Billie Holiday, Duke Ellington, and other music legends.

STUDIO TOURS

Paramount Studios ❹ (5555 Melrose Avenue; tel: 323-956 1777; www.paramountstudios.com; daily tours) is the only major motion-picture studio still located in Hollywood. If peeking in through the wrought-iron gates isn't enough shoulder-rubbing with stardom for you, you can view the back lot on a two-hour or even a four-and-a-half-hour walking tour through the studios, film sets (when not in use), sound stages, and props department, and catch a glimpse of other behind-the-scenes activities. It reveals a peek at such tricks of the trade as the B-tank, where Moses parted the waters in *The Ten Commandments*, and New York Street, a façade of brownstones made of fiberglass and aged to look like real brick. The After Dark Tours are by reservation only, for visitors aged 10 and over.

If you drive west on Melrose from Paramount Studios, you'll arrive at the trendy section of **Melrose Avenue** (between La Brea and Fairfax), where young tourists, local hipsters, and fashionable freaks populate the funky boutiques, restaurants, and cafés.

FAMOUS LAST RESTING PLACES

A few blocks from Paramount is the **Hollywood Forever Cemetery 5** (6000 Santa Monica Boulevard at Gower; tel: 323-469 1181; gate hours: Mon–Fri 8.30am–5pm, summer until 5.30pm), where many stars are buried. The graves of Cecil B. DeMille and Douglas Fairbanks Sr. can be found in the lake area. The Cathedral Mausoleum holds Rudolph Valentino's crypt, which was visited by the mysterious Lady in Black each year on the anniversary of his death, until she died in 1989. For a true LA experience, check out one of the classic movie screenings or concerts the cemetery hosts on its grounds (seasonal; www.cinespia.org, www.hollywoodforever. com/culture).

Hollywood Hike

For breathtaking views of the city and people-watching at its finest, the 3-mile (5-km) loop at Runyon Canyon Park in the heart of Hollywood (2001 N. Fuller Avenue) is a favorite among tourists and Angelenos alike.

The Pierce Brothers Westwood Village Memorial Park (1218 Glendon Avenue; tel: 310-474 1579), a five-minute walk south of Westwood Village, boasts one of the most famous graves in all of Los Angeles, that of Marilyn Monroe. Her former husband, Joe DiMaggio, adorned her simple wall crypt with roses every week for 25 years after her death.

Marble statuary and mammoth artwork spread across both branches of **Forest Lawn Memorial Park** (tel: 800-204 3131; http://forest lawn.com; daily 8am–5pm, until 6pm during daylight savings time). Stan Laurel and Buster Keaton are among those buried in the Hollywood Hills branch, 4 miles (6km) north of Hollywood. Walt Disney, Humphrey Bogart, Spencer Tracy, Elizabeth Taylor and Michael Jackson are just a few of those buried in the Glendale branch, 7 miles (11km) north of Downtown.

La Brea Tar Pits

THE WILSHIRE DISTRICT

Wilshire Boulevard began as an Indian trail connecting the downtown area with the La Brea Tar Pits and later was developed as an upscale shopping and business district. Today it is one of the widest and longest boulevards in North America, showcasing the many faces of Los Angeles. Stretching 16 miles (25km) from Downtown to the sea, it passes through a variety of ethnic neighborhoods and financial brackets – from the very poor to the ridiculously wealthy.

The stretch of Wilshire between La Brea and Fairfax avenues is known as the Mid-Wilshire district or Miracle Mile. It boasts several cultural attractions along its 'Museum Row.'

A fascinating attraction is the **La Brea Tar Pits** ❻, one of the world's richest sources of Pleistocene fossils that date back 40,000 years. In the large pit in front of the Museum, life-size replicas of mastodons are shown trapped in the tar, which was formed by oil deposits collected in pools on the earth's surface. From viewing stations alongside other pits, you can watch the excavations and view the bones of the pre-historic beasts that perished here.

The adjacent **La Brea Tar Pits Museum** (5801 Wilshire Boulevard; tel: 213-763 3499; www.tarpits.org; daily 9.30am–5pm) provides fascinating insight into Ice Age life in southern California. The *Titans of the Ice Age* is an introductory 3D film illustrating how the animals became trapped in the asphalt as they edged down to a pool of water to drink. Skeletons of such extinct creatures as the saber-toothed cat, imperial mammoth, and giant ground sloth have been reconstructed from the fossils. The wall display of 400 wolf skulls brings a startling realization of just how many animals have been unearthed here.

Of the 420 animal species found in the area, only one human fossil has been discovered: the 9,000-year-old La Brea Woman. Killed by a blow to the head, she was perhaps LA's first murder victim. The museum also features a fishbowl laboratory where visitors can see fossils being cleaned and catalogued. The peaceful atrium nurtures primitive plants, several of which have evolved over a period of 100 million years.

After leaving the museum, take the scenic route by making a right on 4th Street off La Brea to admire the splendid homes in Hancock Park residential neighborhood.

MUSEUM ROW

The **Los Angeles County Museum of Art** ❼ (5905 Wilshire Boulevard; tel: 323-857 6000; www.lacma.org; Mon, Tue, Thu 11am–5pm, Fri 11am–8pm, Sat–Sun 10am–7pm), the city's

Farmer's Market and the Grove Shopping Mall

largest museum, is located next door. Among the treasures in this seven-building complex are a collection of pre-Colum- bian artifacts that were found in Mexico and Peru, European modern and contemporary art, American colonial art and furniture, Japanese masterpieces, and what is generally regarded as the finest Indian and Southeast Asian art col- lection in the West. The Broad Contemporary Art Museum at LACMA is the latest addition to the fold, with stunning display space for changing exhibitions of contemporary art (www.the broad.org). The museum is gearing up for a major makeover, which will see four of its old structures replaced by a state- of-the-art building in 2023. Before this, there are plans for a new neighbour onsite with The **Academy Museum of Motion Picture** (www.oscars.org), due to open in 2017. Designed by award-winning architect Renzo Piano, it's sure to become the world's premier movie museum.

The small but extremely significant **Craft and Folk Art Museum** (5814 Wilshire Boulevard; tel: 323-937 4230; www.

cafam.org; Tue–Fri 11am–5pm, Sat–Sun noon–6pm, 1st Tue of each month also 6.30–9.30pm; Sun "pay what you want") rotates exhibitions from around the world.

At 6060 Wilshire at Fairfax is the **Petersen Automotive Museum** (tel: 323-930 2277; www.petersen.org; Tue–Sun 10am–6pm). It celebrates the town's love affair with cars, showcasing over 160 distinctive motor vehicles in new innovative galleries, including interactive children's displays. At the time of writing the museum was preparing for its grand reopening in December 2015, following an extensive remodeling of its three floors and the exterior, which will now be wrapped in ribbons of stainless steel.

A few blocks north on Fairfax is the lively **Farmers' Market** ❽ (6333 West Third Street; tel: 323-933 9211; www.farmers marketla.com; Mon–Fri 9am–9pm, Sat 9am–8pm, Sun 10am–7pm). In the 1930s a small group of Depression-era farmers gathered in what was then a field at the edge of town, to sell produce directly to the people. Its popularity as a meeting place has kept it busy since then, with crowds perusing the fruit and vegetable stands for the best bargains, a maze of shops selling foodstuffs and gifts, and inexpensive food stalls. The upscale outdoor shopping center **The Grove** (323-900 8080; www.thegrovela.com) is directly adjacent, with boutiques and restaurants, a movie theater, choreographed fountains, and even a double-decker trolley for the kids.

THE WESTSIDE

Several communities make up the area collectively known as the 'Westside.' They are linked not only by geographical location but also by image: it is around here that some of the most beautiful people congregate. It's also where the upmarket and fashionable neighborhoods converge, with their affluent residential areas, trendy restaurants, and fabulous shopping areas.

Sunset and Hollywood Boulevard street signs

WEST HOLLYWOOD

While Hollywood is more remembered than experienced, its neighbor **West Hollywood** defines the cutting edge. Within its 2 square miles (5 sq km) are over 100 restaurants, many night-clubs, interior design shops and galleries, swanky hotels, and the offices of the entertainment and music industries.

Melrose Avenue and Beverly and Robertson Boulevards are known as the 'Avenues of Design.' The streets here are lined with design showrooms, fashion boutiques, and art galleries, including the **Pacific Design Center** ❾ (8687 Melrose Avenue; tel: 310-657 0800; www.pacificdesigncenter.com; Mon–Fri 9am–5pm), a gigantic, blue-glass building known as the Blue Whale, designed by Cesar Pelli in 1975. Some 130 showrooms are housed here and in the adjoining Green Center, which dis-plays an impressive range of traditional and contemporary home and office furniture created by famous designers. The latest addition, the Red Building, houses 400,000 sq ft/37,000 sqm of office and retail space and was completed in 2013. The showrooms are for trade only, meaning only interior designers and their clients can browse and buy. You can, however, visit the **MOCA Gallery** (tel: 213-626 6222; www.moca.org; Tue–Fri 11am–5pm, Sat–Sun 11am–6pm; free), a satellite of the Museum of Contemporary Art downtown, which presents temporary exhibitions on design and architecture.

Spanning the length of West Hollywood is **Santa Monica Boulevard** – the center of LA's gay and lesbian nightlife. Every year in June, the city holds LA Pride, a lively three-day festival and parade that has grown into the third largest in California. The street goes wild each Halloween, too.

Sunset Tower Hotel

SUNSET STRIP

West Hollywood's most famous thoroughfare is without a doubt the **Sunset Strip**, stretching from the 8200 block of Sunset Boulevard west to Doheny Drive. Since the 1920s it has been the stomping grounds for LA's partying celebrities. With many renovations dating from the 1990s economic boom, its hotels and clubs remained spectacularly impervious to the recent downturn. Many top comedians started here in clubs such as The Comedy Store (http://thecomedystore. com), while rock'n'roll legends were born in the dance halls of The Roxy (www.the

roxy.com) and Whisky-A-Go-Go (www.whiskyagogo.com). On weekends the Strip's traffic slows as the young and the hip traipse from one nightspot to the next. But even if you never leave your car, the huge billboards beaming with the faces of celebrities promoting their latest movie or recording (or simply themselves) announce this is the town's wild play palace.

Among the landmarks are the **Sunset Tower Hotel ⑩** (8358 Sunset Boulevard; www.sunsettowerhotel.com), a stately Art-Deco masterpiece. Built in 1931, it was the first all-electric apartment building in California, and has been featured in several films. Clark Gable, Errol Flynn, and Jean Harlow were three of the many stars who once lived here. Further west is the **Mondrian** hotel (8440 Sunset Boulevard), with modern décor by Philippe Starck, and a parade of celebrities who frequent the SkyBar cocktail lounge.

Sunset Plaza (8600–8700 Sunset Boulevard at Sunset Plaza Drive; www.sunsetplaza.com), an elite shopping area since 1934, is a cluster of Georgian-style buildings that were designed by Charles Selkirk. Once home to the Mocambo and Trocadero nightclubs, today the plaza is lined with upmarket, one-of-a-kind specialty shops and European-style sidewalk cafés – a top spot for people-watching.

BEVERLY HILLS

Hip gives way to chic at Doheny Drive, where the Strip ends and Sunset Boulevard enters **Beverly Hills**. Here, luxurious homes and landscaped lawns sit on some of the most expensive real estate in the world. It's worth sidetracking into the hills just to marvel at them. On this stretch of Sunset you're bound to find hawkers on street corners selling 'Maps to the Stars' to lead you to the homes of the rich and famous.

This millionaire mecca is a testament to the region's unparalleled success. At the turn of the 20th century the land was practically worthless, covered with failed oil wells and fields of lima beans. But in 1912, when developers built the **Beverly Hills Hotel ⑪** (9641 Sunset Boulevard), everything changed. The Spanish Colonial-style building was soon dubbed the Pink Palace and fast became popular with the movie set. Its Polo Lounge is now a notorious watering hole for Hollywood's power brokers. Marilyn Monroe and John F. Kennedy were said to be among the celebrities who met secretly in the private bungalows. The hotel is now owned by one of the richest men in the world, the Sultan of Brunei, who restored it to its blatant grandeur for a whopping $100 million.

In 1920, silent-screen stars Mary Pickford and Douglas Fairbanks built their opulent estate, Pickfair, just up the hill (at 1143 Summit Drive). Charlie Chaplin, Gloria Swanson, Rudolph Valentino, and others also flocked in to establish one of the most concentrated celebrity enclaves in the world. (The homes 'in the hills' are regarded as somewhat more prestigious than those 'in the flats').

It's not surprising that the highest number of business licenses in Beverly Hills are issued to gardeners. Those who are not busy manicuring the residential lawns are often to be found working in the lovely **Beverly Gardens Park**, which borders Santa Monica Boulevard for 2 miles (3km) from Doheny to Wilshire.

Another stretch of beautiful gardens can be seen at **Greystone Mansion ⑫**, the spectacular neo-Gothic estate of oilman Edward Doheny. Now a city-owned property and frequent film set (eg *Witches of Eastwick*, *Big Lebowski*), the mansion is closed to visitors but the grounds are open daily (905 Loma Vista Drive; tel: 310-285 6830; www.greystonemansion. org; 10am–5pm, Mar–Oct until 6pm; free).

To see the most renowned section of Beverly Hills, take a walk through the elite shopping strip known as **Rodeo Drive ⑬** (pronounced Ro-DAY-oh), where leading designers showcase their fashions to a rich, glamorous and sophisticated clientele. If the likes of Gucci, Hermès, Armani, and Tiffany are outside your budget, at least window-shopping is free. At its southern end, the street meets Wilshire Boulevard at Via Rodeo, a pretty cobblestone stretch designed to look like a European shopping street.

Opposite is the **Beverly Wilshire** (9500 Wilshire Boulevard), a landmark since 1928. The luxury hotel is still a favorite of celebrities and visiting royalty, some of whom rent entire floors for their stay. It's more publicly renowned as the setting where Julia Roberts' and Richard Gere's characters found love in the film *Pretty Woman*.

Nearby is the **Paley Center for Media** (465 N. Beverly Drive; tel: 310-786 1000; www.paleycenter.org; Wed–Sun noon–5pm; donation suggested). Like its counterpart in New York, it

Rodeo Drive

contains a vast archive, with over 120,000 radio and television programs and commercials dating from the early days of broadcasting. Find your favorites and watch them in the screening room, or take in the special exhibits.

The **Beverly Hills Trolley** offers a 40-minute guided tour of landmarks and residential areas for $5 ($1 children 12 and under). Catch it at the southeast corner of Rodeo Drive and Dayton Way (year-round Sat–Sun 11am–4pm; July–Aug and Thanksgiving–Dec Tue–Sun 11am–4pm). For more information, call 310-285 1128 or visit www.beverlyhills.org.

CENTURY CITY

Though there is not much to see at **Century City**, it's worth noting that this complex of buildings was built on 180 acres (73 hectares) of what was once Twentieth Century Fox's enormous back-lot studio. The motion picture studio, now relegated to a huge compound on Pico Boulevard, is still active and churning out productions. But the surrounding area is a sleek Westside business center of high-rise office towers, high-flying corporations, theaters, and shops set around the striking, silver Century City Towers. If you find yourself with time to kill in this area, the **Westfield Century City** (10250 Santa Monica Boulevard; www.westfield.com/centurycity) outdoor shopping center offers department stores, upscale boutiques, an elegant food court, and a state-of-the-art movie theater. New to the area are the offices of the respected **Santa Monica Museum of Art** (www.smmoa.org), which no longer features a permanemt collection. As part of its SMMoA Unbound phase, pop-up exhibitions will take place at different sites through the city.

Opened in 1993, the **Museum of Tolerance** ⑮ (9786 West Pico Boulevard; tel: 310-553 84032505; www.museumoftolerance.com; Mon–Fri 10am–5pm, Nov–Mar Fri until 3.30pm, Sun 10am–5pm, Thu until 9.30pm for "Anne"; last admission 1.5 hours

The University of California, Los Angeles

before closing, check website for closures on Jewish holidays; bring photo ID; advance reservations recommended) is a chilling and provocative experience, with impressive high-tech exhibits exploring racism and prejudice in America and elsewhere. A major part is devoted to *Hashoah*, the Holocaust. Visitors are given the 'passport' of a real person who experienced the concentration camps, which are depicted in film footage, sets, and interviews. This tour alone lasts a full hour, and at least equal time is necessary to appreciate the other collections, including a remarkable multimedia exhibit on the life and legacy of Anne Frank, and the learning center on the second floor.

WESTWOOD, BEL AIR, AND BRENTWOOD

The sprawling campus of the **University of California, Los Angeles ⑯** (UCLA) dominates Westwood. The grounds, with lovely Royce Hall dating from 1929, Powell Library, Franklin Murphy Sculpture Garden (with works by Matisse, Rodin, and Miró), and the Mathias Botanical Gardens, offer a respite from the motor metropolis. Information is available from the kiosks in Westwood Boulevard, Westholme Avenue and Charles E. Young Drive; ask for the free 90-minute campus walking tours during the week (tel: 310-825 4321; www.ucla.edu/visit).

To the south of the campus, **Westwood Village** is an area that was once a hub of social activity but suffered a decline due to the revitalization of Santa Monica's Third Street Promenade. Today it's still a popular place to catch the latest film at any of the theaters or cruise the shops and restaurants. At the village's southern tip, the **Hammer Museum** (10899 Wilshire Boulevard; tel: 310-443 7000; www.hammer.ucla.edu; Tue–Fri 11am–8pm, Sat–Sun 11am–5pm; free) presents a small but exquisite collection of artwork gathered over a period of 50 years by the great industrialist Armand Hammer. Its galleries display masterpieces by painters from Rembrandt to Van Gogh, with an extensive collection of lithographs by Honoré Daumier. The museum regularly hosts special exhibitions.

To the north of UCLA, across Sunset Boulevard, is the exclusive neighborhood of **Bel Air**. As the tight-knit community is an enclave of old-money estates for such notables as the Reagans, you won't get to glimpse more than big front gates and lawns. You can, however, get a peek into the good life at **Hotel Bel-Air**'s ⓱ restaurant, lounge, and gardens (701 Stone Canyon Road), where celebs often linger.

The LA art world's star attraction is the **Getty Center** ⓲, the visual-arts complex designed by Richard Meier and perched on a bluff high above the 405 freeway in Brentwood, just west of UCLA. The cost: a whopping one billion dollars. Opened in 1998, the Center comprises the **J. Paul Getty Museum** (1200 Getty Center Drive; tel: 310-440 7300; www.getty.edu; Tue–Fri and Sun 10am–5.30pm, Sat 10am–9pm; free, parking fee) plus institutes for arts education, conservation, and research. The museum has a major collection of Western art from the

J. Paul Getty Museum

Middle Ages to the present day, with European paintings (by Rembrandt, Monet, Renoir, and Van Gogh, among others), drawings (including a few by Michelangelo, Leonardo da Vinci, and Raphael), illuminated medieval manuscripts, photographs, sculpture, and French decorative arts displayed within five two-story pavilions.

The impressive architecture, central gardens (designed by California artist Robert Irwin), and panoramic views of city, mountains, and ocean are awesome attractions in themselves. Take in the beautiful scenery by either dining in the museum's elegant restaurant, outdoor café, or by ordering a picnic lunch (tel: 310-440 6213) to enjoy alfresco on the beautiful grounds.

North of the Getty Center, the **Skirball Cultural Center** ⑲ (2701 N. Sepulveda Boulevard; tel: 310-440 4500; www.skirball. org; Tue–Fri noon–5pm, Sat–Sun 10am–5pm, check the website for closures on Jewish holidays; charge, free on Thu) depicts Jewish heritage and immigration, from ancient times to beginning life in America.

COASTAL LOS ANGELES

From Malibu in the north to Long Beach in the south, the shoreline communities of Los Angeles County stretch for 72 miles (115km) along the striking edge of the ocean.

   Driving north on Pacific Coast Highway 1 (often marked 'PCH') from Santa Monica to Malibu is an excellent introduction to southern California's seductive beach life. Palos Verdes Drive is another eye-catching stretch, hugging the cliffs along the southern tip of Santa Monica Bay. But to really appreciate the allure of the California lifestyle, you must ditch the car and hit the sand and experience the natural beauty of the beaches first hand.

SANTA MONICA TO MARINA DEL REY

Ever since it was founded in the 1870s, **Santa Monica** has been thought of as the perfect seaside town. Nonetheless, in the

Overlooking the beach from Santa Monica Pier

1930s poker games, bingo parlors, and a casino barge anchored offshore brought such notoriety to the area that author Raymond Chandler used Santa Monica as the model for the freewheeling 'Bay City' of his detective novels. Today, with trendy boutiques, blue-chip art galleries, a buzzing nightlife scene, and some of the finest restaurants in the county, Santa Monica looks as if it is set to continue forever as LA's most popular playground.

Murals

Santa Monica and Venice Beach have dozens of murals, including 'Venice Reconstituted,' with Botticelli's Venus on roller skates. The half-mile long Great Wall of Los Angeles is another noteworthy site. For more information, contact the Social and Public Art Resource Center at 685 Venice Boulevard (tel: 310-822 9560; www.sparcmurals.org).

Santa Monica Pier ⓴, site of the famous carousel as well as the former La Monica Ballroom, was built in 1908. Much of this historic structure was demolished by storms in 1983, prompting restoration to its original look. While the arcades and amusement park rides lining the pier lure tourists with their wonderfully tacky old-world ambiance, locals also come here to rent fishing tackle at the end of the pier or check out the festive free concerts held each summer. Beneath the pier and as far as the eye can see to the north and south you'll find beachgoers at play on the widest band of sand on the Pacific Coast. The busy path running alongside the beach to Venice is a coveted track for cyclists and rollerbladers, who either bring their own gear or rent from the numerous establishments nearby.

Above the sand is **Palisades Park**, a pretty, palm-lined stretch that runs for a mile (1.5km) along Ocean Avenue. Though it has become a notorious gathering place for the city's homeless population, it's worth strolling the broad walkway for its superb views of the ocean. Just inland you'll find Santa Monica's **Main Street**, which is awash with unusual shops and excellent restaurants. Looming over its southern end at the intersection with Rose Avenue is a giant sculpture by Jonathan Borofsky known as *Ballerina Clown*. As its name implies, this is a giant clown's head on a tutu-clad body.

The **Edgemar complex**, located in the 2400 block, was designed by renowned postmodern architect Frank Gehry, a Santa Monica resident. Inside is a restaurant, retail shops, offices, and cinemas. Santa Monica artists also mount shows

BEST BEACHES

Angelenos converge all along the coast in a veritable beach party of surfers, volleyball players, families, skaters, bikers, bodybuilders, and bathing beauties.

Malibu's Surfrider Beach has some of the best surfing around. **Santa Monica Beach** and **Venice Beach** are two of the most popular, with a wealth of activities on the boardwalk and pleasure pier.

South Bay beaches – Manhattan, Hermosa, and Redondo – are where California's beach culture started when George Freeth first caught the waves at Redondo Beach in 1907. The Beach Boys immortalized the surfer's life here in song in the 1960s.

Long Beach has an extensive 5.5 miles (9km) of beach, with numerous water sports and activities.

Orange County has some of the area's best beaches.

Bolsa Chica State Beach is a beautiful 6-mile (9.5km) stretch adjoining a wetlands reserve. Its gentle surf makes it good for families. Adjacent **Huntington Beach** is one of the world's great surfing spots.

Newport Beach and **Balboa Beach**, joined by a busy bike path, are the most popular spots on this part of the coast.

Main Beach lies smack in the middle of town in Laguna Beach, and the wooden boardwalk rivals few others as a vantage spot.

A PERFECT TOUR

Days 1–4

North Aegean

Pick up a hire car in İstanbul, drive to Gallipoli, spending the night in Kocadere. The next day, finish touring the peninsula's World War I battlefields, crossing to Çanakkale for lunch. Drive to Troy in the afternoon, then cross to Bozcaada and stay overnight. Return to the mainland, arriving at Assos for lunch and to see the ancient acropolis. Continue to Ayvalık or Cunda for dinner and hotel. In the morning, go to Pergamon's acropolis and Asklepion, lunching at Foça en route to Alaçatı.

Day 10

Day in Dalyan

The following day, head east to Dalyan for lunch and İztuzu beach (by car). Next morning, take a river cruise to nearby hot springs and ancient Kaunos.

Days 5–6

On to Ephesus

Take the coast road to Kuşadası for a two-night stay. Spend the afternoon at Ephesus and visiting the Selçuk museum. The next day go to Pamukkale.

Days 7–9

Ephesus to Knidos

Head south, via ancient Priene, Miletus and Didyma, towards Bodrum, stopping for lunch at Milas' port of Iassos. Arrive at Bodrum (or a peninsula resort) for two nights' stay. There's time for windsurfing, diving or just idling in the bazaar. Get an early start, pausing for Muğla's historic houses, en route to Datça; swim at an excellent beach to the west, with Knidos left for sunset.

BODRUM CASTLE
The massive Crusader Castle is home to treasures salvaged from the deep. See page 53.

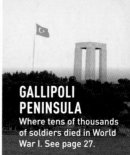

GALLIPOLI PENINSULA
Where tens of thousands of soldiers died in World War I. See page 27.

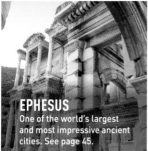

EPHESUS
One of the world's largest and most impressive ancient cities. See page 45.

AYVALIK
A remarkably intact late Ottoman Greek town. See page 33.

ASPENDOS
A Roman theatre with an annual opera and ballet festival. See page 79.

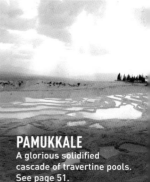

PAMUKKALE
A glorious solidified cascade of travertine pools. See page 51.

in the second-floor galleries of the **California Heritage Museum** ㉑ (2612 Main Street; tel: 310-392 8537; www.cali forniaheritagemuseum.org; Wed–Sun 11am–4pm). This former American Colonial home was moved to Main Street, and its lower floor has been restored to reflect a turn-of-the-20th-century lifestyle.

Beach volleyball is a popular sport

Dozens of prominent art galleries have set up shop in Santa Monica, with the result that it is now a major center of the contemporary art scene. Many shops are situated along a stretch of Colorado Avenue between 9th and 10th streets.

Aside from the beach, the **Third Street Promenade** ㉒ has become the most popular destination in Santa Monica. This three-block pedestrian mall, with its street performers, dinosaur topiaries, shops, movie houses, and restaurants, is perennially teeming with tourists and locals, especially on weekend evenings, when the pubs, pool halls, cafés, and shops guarantee an action-packed night out.

Curiously enough, Santa Monica has a large contingent of British residents, evident in the authentic pubs such as Ye Olde King's Head (complete with dart boards; www.yeolde kingshead.com), just off the Promenade. Roughly 10 percent of the city's residents are of British descent and there's an active expat community with organised events.

Further inland is the shopping street of **Montana Avenue**, where celebrities living in the coastal enclaves come to shop

A surfer cycles along Venice Beach

(see page 86). Santa Monica Airport's **Museum of Flying** ㉓, reopened in 2012 in a new building, displays vintage planes (tel: 310-398 2500; www.museumofflying.org; Wed–Sun 10am–5pm), and **Bergamot Station** (2525 Michigan Avenue), a converted trolley-car station, has an Art Center housing a number of commercial art galleries.

Just south of Rose Avenue, Main Street abruptly enters the bohemian community of **Venice Beach** ㉔. While cottages are scattered along small, quaint residential side streets, the Ocean Front Walk is an explosion of exuberance, with an ongoing parade of outrageous characters exhibiting their only-in-southern-California individualism. It's worth a stroll just to check out the freaks and the musclemen pumping iron at the open-air beachside gym known as Muscle Beach, but the sidewalk artists, snack shacks, T-shirt vendors, and Tarot readers also contribute to the local flavor. The show is at its best on weekend afternoons, with everything from beach boys on unicycles to rock musicians on roller blades. Make time for this California happening if you possibly can. Nearby boho-chic **Abbot Kinney Boulevard** ㉕ (http://abbotkinneyblvd.com), with its hip boutiques, eclectic restaurants, and cutting-edge art galleries, is a worthwhile excursion as well.

Everything mellows out at Mother's Beach to the south, a lagoon specifically preferred by families, and becomes ultra-civilized at the vast man-made harbor of **Marina del Rey** (www.visitmarinadelrey.com), where harbor cruises and fishing trips can be arranged. Fisherman's Village on Fiji Way attracts tourists with gift shops and cafés. But if you just want to watch the yachts and other water craft, you should be able to find a shady spot along Mindanao Way at Burton Chase Park.

NORTH TO MALIBU

To the north of Santa Monica, PCH meets the western terminus of Sunset Boulevard. Follow this winding road into the hills and you will find yourself in the well-to-do residential enclave of the Pacific Palisades. Located a few miles farther on Sunset Boulevard is the turn-off for **Will Rogers State Historic Park** (1501 Will Rogers State Park Road; free, parking fee), a 186-acre (75-hectare) ranch that belonged to the late cowboy humorist. Tours of the ranch house (tel: 310-454 8212 ext.100; www.parks.ca.gov/willrogers; Thu–Fri 11am–3pm, Sat–Sun 10am–4pm on the hour) reveal some of Rogers' eccentricities, namely a porch swing in the living room and a raised ceiling that allowed him to practice rope tricks indoors. Rogers was an enthusiastic horseman and an experienced polo player. Weekend games are still held on the polo field in the front yard. A good system of hiking trails extends into the park.

A deeply centering experience comes free with a stroll through the **Self-Realization Fellowship Lake Shrine** (17190 Sunset Boulevard, a few blocks before PCH; www.lakeshrine. org; tours Fri and Sun at 3pm). Adjoining the temple (founded by Swami P. Yogananda) is a beautiful garden with gazebos, lakes, and waterfalls.

Malibu is best known for its exclusive beachfront colonies, home to movie stars since the 1930s. You'll get to see only the backs of these expensive bungalows as you travel its 21 miles (34km) on the ribbon of highway that lies between the mountains and the sea. Some homes have been destroyed by the brush fires and mudslides that periodically threaten this area. There are several beach access points where you can still admire the rolling surf and idyllic beach life that have made Malibu famous. One such is **Malibu Pier** (23000 Pacific Coast Highway), a popular spot for fishing. Constructed in 1905 and rebuilt several times since, this was the main connection with the south until the state highway was built in 1929. More recent additions include water-sports rentals and whale-watching and

The Getty Villa

harbor tours. Another is **Malibu Lagoon State Beach**, one of the few remaining wetlands in California. Several board-walks extend into the marsh, where you can see shorebirds such as the great blue heron and American avocet. A popu-lar surfing beach adjoins the lagoon, as does the historic **Adamson House**, a Spanish-style mansion and museum decorated wall-to-wall with colorful ceramic tiles (23200 Pacific Coast Highway; tel: 310-456 8432; www.adamson house.org; Fri–Sat 11am–3pm, last tour at 2pm, Tue bus tour only).

The **Getty Villa**, with its classical architecture and stun-ning courtyard pool, is one of the coastline's most popular attractions (17985 Pacific Coast Highway; tel: 310-440 7300; www.getty.edu; Wed–Mon 10am–5pm; free, advanced timed tickets are required and can be reserved by phone or online; parking fee). Formerly known as the J. Paul Getty Museum (now at the Getty Center; see page 44), it opened in 1954 to house the billionaire's personal collection. The museum's 1974 addition was a re-creation of Villa dei Papiri, a Roman villa destroyed by the eruption of Mount Vesuvius in AD79. After a major nine-year restoration, the villa reopened in 2006 and is once more a fitting home for the outstanding collection of Greek, Roman, and Etruscan antiquities, dating back to 3000BC.

DOWNTOWN

For the majority of the residents of Los Angeles, 'Downtown' is not a hub but a distant skyline visited a few times a year when attending the opera or going to the Museum of Contemporary Art. But that's not to say the region east of Hollywood, which is defined by three freeways and the river, doesn't have its mer-its. A core of beautiful historic buildings, good restaurants, and colorful ethnic enclaves makes for excellent daytime

Strolling on Olvera Street

exploration. Several stellar performing arts venues and the centers of politics and finance also draw attention. This is a lively workaday business world, with hotels overflowing with conventioneers, and an atmosphere that is a refreshing diversion from the celluloid images to the west. Ten years ago, the place was all but a ghost town come night-time but thanks to an influx of hipster residents, hot bars, and trendy restaurants, these days it's is a hub of happening nightlife.

By day, Downtown is best explored on foot and on the DASH buses, which run through the area during the day for just 50 cents a ride (www.ladottransit.com/dash). By nightfall, when thousands of commuters return to the suburbs and the streets are more deserted (despite Downtown's recent revival, it's still no New York City), it's best to drive or take a cab. As in any large city, simple precautions are recommended.

One of the best ways to appreciate the area is to take one of the excellent walking tours given on Saturdays by the Los Angeles Conservancy. The Historic Downtown Tour is highly recommended. A variety of special-interest tours are also offered, including Art Deco or Downtown Renaissance. For information, call 213-623 2489 on weekdays between 9am and 5pm, or visit www.laconservancy.org.

LANDMARK BUILDINGS

At 5th and Figueroa, the five cylindrical towers of glass at the **Westin Bonaventure Hotel** form the city's most futuristic skyscraper (www.thebonaventure.com). Survey the area from the revolving restaurant and bar on the 35th floor. To the east at 630 West 5th Street, between Grand Avenue and Flower Street, is the pyramid-topped **Central Library** ㉖ (tel: 213-228 7000, tours: 213-228 7168; www.lapl.org/central; Mon–Thu 10am–8pm, Fri–Sat 9.30am–5.30pm, Sun 1–5pm). Built in 1926, it was devastated by fire 60 years later but was restored to its original design by 1993. On the second floor are murals of California history by Dean Cornwell and literary exhibits in the Getty Gallery. Free tours (no reservations necessary for groups of six or less) are given Mon–Fri at 12.30pm, Sat at 11am and 2pm, Sun at 2pm. On Saturdays at 12.30pm, there is also an art tour available of the library's Maguire Gardens.

Across from the library is the 73-story, 1,018ft (310m) **US Bank Tower** ㉗ (an office building formerly known as the Library Tower), the tallest building on the West Coast, designed by I.M. Pei. A rooftop observation deck is due to open to the public in 2016 as part of the building's $50 million makeover. Running alongside, the majestic **Bunker Hill Steps** lead to California Plaza, forming a symbolic link between the old Downtown and the new.

The **Millennium Biltmore** (506 South Grand Avenue; tel: 213-624 1011; www.thebiltmore.com), opened in 1923, is the *grande dame* of all the Downtown hotels. The Academy Awards were launched here in a private ceremony in the

Crystal Room in 1927. The majestic Rendezvous Court near Olive Street was originally the hotel lobby; from here, you can climb the Spanish baroque staircase leading up to the galleria, with its coffered ceiling.

On the other side of Olive Street, the landscaped **Pershing Square** is the city's oldest public park. Its history as a public commons dates back to 1781.

Art Deco is at its best in the nearby **Oviatt Building** (617 South Olive Street; http://oviatt.com). In 1927, merchant James Oviatt was entranced with the new architectural style that he saw in Paris. He subsequently commissioned René Lalique to design all the decorative glass for his building, which was home to his haberdashery and penthouse suite.

Some of Downtown's landmark buildings

From its terminal on 3rd and Hill streets, the **Angel's Flight** (http://angelsflight.com) inclined railway carried Downtowners up and down Bunker Hill beginning in 1901. After a fatal accident in 2001, the funicular railway was suspended, but it reopened in 2010. It's currently closed again, dealing with regulatory issues. So until it's back up and running, those wishing to get to **California Plaza**, a good spot to eat lunch outdoors, will need to tackle some steep steps.

BROADWAY AND THE CIVIC CENTER

The historic theater district on Broadway has evolved into a bustling Latino shopping street good for bridal gowns and electronic equipment. However, one monument to its past is the **Million Dollar Theater** (307 South Broadway; tel: 213-617 3600; www.milliondollar.la) with its wonderful, whimsical terracotta ornamentation. This famous 1917 vaudeville and movie theater, renovated, features classic film screenings and live Latino acts ('*variedades*').

Built in 1893, the lovely **Bradbury Building** ❷ (at 304 South Broadway) is Los Angeles' oldest commercial building. It is also one of the grandest, with fancy Victorian wrought-iron balconies, marble staircases, and open-cage elevators surrounding a skylit atrium court. Both the Bradbury Building and the Million Dollar Theater, as well as the Angel's Flight and the Millennium Biltmore, are featured on the Historic Downtown tours run on Saturdays by the Los Angeles Conservancy (tel: 213-623 2489; www.laconservancy.org).

Since 1917, **Grand Central Market** (317 South Broadway; www.grandcentralmarket.com; daily 9am–6pm, Thu–Sat until 9pm; free) has provided the city with a daily cornucopia of enticing fresh produce, fish, poultry, meat, and exotic foodstuffs. Today, dozens of stalls display a wonderful ethnic diversity: you can sample everything from fresh tortillas to Chinese herbs. It's a great place for browsing and a quick snack or inexpensive lunch.

The streets around the Civic Center (the area bordered by First and Temple streets, and North Main Street and North Grand Avenue) are the heart of Los Angeles culture and politics. **City Hall** ❷ (200 N. Spring Street; www.lacity.org/for-visitors), built in 1928, was the tallest building in the city until height restrictions were lifted in 1957. Best known as the *Daily Planet* building of the *Superman* TV series, its observation

Union Station

deck is open weekdays 8am–5pm; free; bring photo ID.

DOWNTOWN REVIVAL

Two more recent attractions form the centerpiece of Downtown's post-millennium revival. **The Cathedral of Our Lady of the Angels** (555 W. Temple Street; tel: 213-680 5200; www.olacathedral.org; Mon–Fri 6.30am–6pm, Sat 9am–6pm, Sun 7am–6pm; free) opened in 2002 with a controversial design by Spanish architect José Rafael Moneo. The sober façade of ochre-colored concrete is surrounded by gardens and a plaza. Bronze doors with multicultural art open into the airy interior lined with tapestries. Free guided tours are given at 1pm weekdays.

The **Music Center** (135 N. Grand Avenue; www.musiccenter. org) is the city's premier venue for the performing arts. Its four theaters (see page 94) were joined in 2003 by the **Walt Disney Concert Hall**, a magnificent stainless-steel building designed by Frank Gehry. There are tours available of its impressive interior (days and times vary, tel: 213-972 7483 or see website). Facing the concert hall is a brand new contemporary art museum called **the Broad** (tel: 213- 232 6220; www. thebroad.org). Two floors of gallery space bathed in diffuse light showcase nearly 2,000 works of art, and the state-of-the-art building is also home to the Broad Art Foundation, run by philanthropists Eli and Edythe Broad. Adjacent to the museum is a new outdoor public plaza. Part of the revitalization project of the area is also the **Grand Park** stretching between the City Hall and the Music Center which opened in 2012.

HISTORIC LOS ANGELES

LA's first settlement in 1781 was at **El Pueblo de Los Angeles**, a state historic park at North Main Street and Paseo de la Plaza. The district's heart is **Olvera Street ㉚**, a festive marketplace brimming with *piñatas* (hanging decorations filled with toys and candy), masks, and Mexican handicrafts, and surrounded by numerous Mexican restaurants and food stalls. The visitors' center (in Avila Adobe, Olvera Street E-25; www.olvera-street.com) provides information on the historical sites of the district, including the **Avila Adobe** (the first house in Los Angeles), the **Old Plaza Church**, and the shady plaza with its wrought-iron gazebo. Free tours are given Tue–Sat at 10am, 11am and noon. *Mariachi* singers and folk dance groups can usually be seen here on weekends.

In a region that long ago eschewed train travel, railway romance still permeates **Union Station** (800 N. Alameda Street). This handsome 1939 Spanish Mission-style building has a massive waiting room with arched corridors and a 52ft (16m) ceiling. The station once served nearly a million passengers a day; now, it is LA's new Metro Rail system hub.

LA'S ASIAN COMMUNITIES

Although Asian Americans live throughout Los Angeles County, there are several special cultural and shopping enclaves that deserve visitors' particular attention.

Chinatown is bounded by the 1000 block of North Broadway and bordered by Ord, Alameda, Bernard, and Yale streets. Here restaurants, souvenir shops, *dim sum* parlors, and

Chinese grocers fan out from the central pedestrian mall (Gin Ling Way). The **Chinese American Museum** (425 N. Los Angeles Street; tel: 213-485 8567; www.camla.org; Tue–Sun 10am–3pm; donation suggested) has exhibits ranging from historical photos to contemporary local artworks.

It's worth noting, however, that for truly authentic Chinese cuisine, Angelenos who are in the know head 10 miles northeast of Downtown to the **San Gabriel Valley**, home to the largest concentration of Chinese-Americans in the US.

The Japanese counterpart, **Little Tokyo**, is situated east of Downtown on the streets around 1st and Central. A medieval fire tower marks the entrance to the Japanese Village Plaza shopping mall (335 East 2nd Street; www.japanesevillageplaza.net). Other community highlights are a cultural center, a theater, and the **Japanese American National Museum** (100 North Central Avenue; tel: 213-625 0414; www.janm.org; Tue, Wed, Fri–Sun

Little Tokyo, Japanese cultural center

11am–5pm, Thu noon–8pm; free Thu after 5pm and 3rd Thu of each month all day), which presents changing exhibits in a Buddhist temple. A third Asian neighborhood, **Koreatown**, lies west of Downtown along Olympic Boulevard between Vermont and Western avenues. All the signs are in Korean, and there is a multitude of restaurants and a shopping mall of Korean stores at Koreatown Plaza (Western and San Marino).

DOWNTOWN MUSEUMS

The **Museum of Contemporary Art ⓷**, known as MOCA (250 S. Grand Avenue; tel: 213-626 6222; www.moca.org; Mon and Fri 11am–5pm, Thu 11am–8pm, Sat–Sun 11am–6pm; free Thu after 5pm), is one of Los Angeles' most exciting museums, presenting major contemporary shows and a rotating permanent collection by such artists as Piet Mondrian, Mark Rothko, and Franz Kline. There's a superb gift shop on the premises. The museum's interesting annex, the Geffen Contemporary, is a few blocks away in Little Tokyo (at 152 North Central Avenue; same hours as MOCA) and features zany installations, multi-media, and the last 60 years of the museum's permanent collection.

Exposition Park, south of the central downtown area near the campus of the University of Southern California, is the site of several museums and attractions, including the Los Angeles Memorial Coliseum and Sports Arena (www.la coliseum.com).

Natural History Museum ⓷ (900 Exposition Boulevard; tel: 213-763 3466; www.nhm.org; daily 9.30am–5pm; free on select Tues, see website) fans will enjoy its dinosaur skeletons and other fossils. Among the highlights of some three dozen galleries are dioramas of animals in their natural habitats, an impressive mounted megamouth shark, a collection of pre-Columbian artifacts, major exhibits on American history, and the Hall of Birds, with an animated rainforest. The museum's Discovery Center has excellent hands-on displays and activities for children.

The **California Science Center and IMAX Theater** (700 Exposition Park Drive; tel: 323-724 3623; www.california sciencecenter.org; daily 10am–5pm; free except IMAX and special exhibits, parking fee) presents technological exhibits from robotics and fiber optics to a miniature winery. Planes, rockets, and space probes are the focus of the center's Air and Space Gallery. Since 2012 the center has been home to the space shuttle Endeavour, which is now the museum's biggest draw.

Rotating exhibitions on the African-American experience in the United States are offered at the **California African-American Museum** (600 State Drive; tel: 213-744 7432; www. caamuseum.org; Tue–Sat 10am–5pm, Sun 11am–5pm; free, parking fee), which has become a showcase for black history and culture.

THE MOUNTAINS AND VALLEYS

When Angelenos refer to 'The Valley,' they are talking about the San Fernando Valley, a chain of communities north across the mountains from western and downtown Los Angeles. Although it's also home to such major film and television studios – in Burbank and Glendale – as Universal, Warner Brothers, and NBC, the Valley is forever battling its reputation as a boring and actionless suburbia. The nearby San Gabriel Valley is also separated from the Los Angeles basin by a range of mountains.

GRIFFITH PARK

An enticing reason to head to the hills is to visit one of the country's largest urban parks, **Griffith Park**, which separates Burbank and Glendale from Hollywood and covers over 4,000 acres (1,620 hectares). There are several entrances to the park; you can pick up a map at the visitors' center near the eastern

Overlooking Los Angeles from the Griffith Observatory

entrance (4730 Crystal Springs Drive; www.laparks.org/dos/parks/griffithpk), off the Golden State Freeway (Highway 5).

Perhaps the best view of LA can be seen on clear days and nights from the **Griffith Observatory** ㉝ (tel: 213-473 0800; http://griffithobservatory.org; Wed–Fri noon–10pm, Sat–Sun 10am–10pm; free, charge for shows in the planetarium) on Mount Hollywood, a location also featured in the classic James Dean movie *Rebel Without a Cause*. Evening visitors can usually look at the heavens through the Zeiss telescope, a 12-inch (30-cm) refracting telescope that more people have looked through than any other telescope in the world. The Planetarium Theater presents astronomical shows.

The **Los Angeles Zoo & Botanical Gardens** (5333 Zoo Drive, tel: 323-644 4200; www.lazoo.org; daily 10am–5pm), on the northeastern side of the park, harbors more than 400 different species of animals, birds, and reptiles, grouped according to their continental region. The zoo is known for its extensive breeding program for endangered species.

The park is also home to the **Autry National Center** (4700 Western Heritage Way; tel: 323-667 2000; https://theautry. org;Tue–Fri 10am–4pm, Sat–Sun 11am–5pm; free 2nd Tue of each month), a museum dedicated to the diversity and history of the people of the American West. Formerly known as the Autry Museum of Western Heritage, it was founded by Gene Autry, who rode the range in films from the 1930s to the 1950s. His tribute to the 'Wild West' features an impressive collection of historical artifacts, furniture, and art, as well as examples of how the West was romanticized in the arts, literature, film, and advertising. The museum also includes the former collection of the renowned **Southwest Museum of the American Indian**, which merged with the Autry in 2003. The collection represents Native American cultures from Alaska to South America and includes pre-Columbian pottery and textiles, making it one of the most important of its kind. Highlights of

Universal Studios

the collection are on view on Saturdays 10am–4pm in the Historic Southwest Museum Mt. Washington Campus (234 Museum Drive; tel: 323-221 2164; free).

In addition to the above attractions, the park also offers 53 miles (85km) of hiking and horseback riding trails. Perhaps the most popular (though challenging) trail

Mulholland Drive

One reason to head north is to do as the Harley Davidson motorcycle enthusiasts do: cruise Mulholland Drive, a scenic road that twists and turns through the mountains from Highway 101 to Ventura County. It is especially beautiful at night, when the lights of the city shimmer below.

is the one that leads right up to the famous 'Hollywood' sign on Mount Lee. The sign itself is fenced off to visitors, but the views from Mount Lee alone may make the trek worth it.

SAN FERNANDO VALLEY

In addition to seeing one of California's original missions, you'll want to visit this valley to see the movie studios.

The area's biggest draw is **Universal Studios Hollywood** ❹ (off the Hollywood 101 Freeway at either the Universal Center Drive or the Lankershim Boulevard exits; tel: 800-864 8377 or 800-UNIVERSAL; www.universalstudioshollywood.com; daily, hours vary by season). It combines a real working studio and behind-the-scenes tours with amusement park attractions. Visitors can board a tram that travels through famous film sets. Along the way you are attacked by the killer shark from *Jaws* and survive a collapsing bridge, a flash flood, and a bone-shaking simulated 8.3 earthquake. You are then free to explore the magic of Hollywood in attractions such as Jurassic Park: The Ride, a great log-flume ride that ends with a sudden drop; Shrek: 4-D, a cinematic fairytale adventure that puts you in the action; WaterWorld, where the movie comes to life in a wave of spectacular stunts and explosions; the horrifying Revenge of the Mummy ride; and King Kong 360 3-D, an intense immersive ride that puts you in the middle of a pack of carnivorous dinosaurs and the beast himself. The Wizarding World of Harry Potter theme park, which has been a smash hit in Orlando, is due to open in spring 2016. Although the queues for major attractions are often long, musical street shows are always close by to entertain.

Nearby is **CityWalk** (100 Universal City Plaza, Universal City; tel: 818-622 9841; www.citywalkhollywood.com; hours vary by season), a fantasy mall, where whimsical shops and fun, informal restaurants compete for tourist dollars.

Monument at Mission San Fernando Rey de España

Nothing is staged just for the guests at the **Warner Brothers Studios** (3400 Warner Blvd, Burbank; tel: 877-492 8687; www.wbstudio tour.com; daily 7.30am–4pm, summer until 5.30pm). Here the two-hour Studio Tour changes every weekday, depending on shooting schedules, as small groups of guests over eight years of age walk through the back lot past TV and movie sets and tour production facilities. If scheduling allows, guests are permitted to watch rehearsals and the filming of TV shows.

One of California's finest missions lies in northern San

Fernando Valley. The **Mission San Fernando Rey de España** (15151 San Fernando Mission Boulevard, Mission Hills; tel: 818-361 0186 www.mission tour.org/sanfernando; daily 9am–4.30pm), built in 1797,

WaterWorld

With its set based on the film of the same name starring Kevin Costner, Universal's WaterWorld has plenty of thrills, spills, and pyrotechnics.

was named for King Ferdinand III of Spain. The complex includes the workshops, the convent with its Roman arches and painted Indian motifs, and the church with gold-leafed *reredos* (ornamental screens).

PASADENA AND THE SAN GABRIEL VALLEY

Northeast of Downtown you'll find that although the citrus groves that blossomed in the San Gabriel Valley 100 years ago have all but disappeared, this prosperous suburban area still has many botanical delights. The **Los Angeles County Arboretum & Botanic Garden** (301 North Baldwin Avenue, Arcadia; tel: 626-821 3222; www.arboretum.org; daily 9am–5pm; free on 3rd Tue of each month) nurtures plants from around the world. Stretching along the lower slopes of the San Gabriel Mountains, the **Descanso Gardens** (1418 Descanso Drive, La Cañada; tel: 818-949 4200; www.descansogardens. org; daily 9am–5pm) are known for their camellia displays and historic collections of roses.

The wealthiest of California's Spanish missions was the fourth to be built in the chain, **Mission San Gabriel Arcangel** (428 S. Mission Drive, San Gabriel; tel: 626-457 3035; www. sangabrielmissionchurch.org; Mon–Sat 9am–4.30pm, Sun 10am–4pm). The chapel, museum, winery, gardens, and cemetery are open to the public daily.

South of the often snowcapped San Gabriel Mountains is the charming city of **Pasadena**, which has remained true to

Pasadena City Hall at night

its Native American Indian name meaning 'Crown of the Valley.' Attracted by its balmy weather and luscious orange groves, Midwesterners flocked here in the 1880s. Development was fast, and, by the turn of the 20th century, grand mansions and hotels had been built for those vacationing during the winter. Pasadena soon became a popular resort area.

This legacy is apparent in the handsome homes strung along the wide, shaded boulevards and in the grand dome of **Pasadena City Hall** (100 N. Garfield Avenue), built in 1927. The stretch of Colorado Boulevard nearby forms the heart of **Old Town Pasadena**. These 11 blocks are full of historic Victorian buildings that have been restored, and the area has been converted into a bustling shopping and dining district. Of Pasadena's highly reputed buildings, none is more famous than the **Gamble House** (4 Westmoreland Place; tel: 626-793 3334; www.gamblehouse.org; Thu–Sat 10am–3pm, Sun noon–3pm for 1-hour guided tours). Built in 1908 by Charles and Henry Greene, it is a masterpiece of the Arts and Crafts Movement that flourished at the turn of the 20th century. Every detail, from the hand-rubbed fine woods and original furniture to the Tiffany windows and light fixtures, was custom designed for David and Mary Gamble (of Proctor and Gamble fame).

Another architectural highlight is the **Fenyes Mansion** (470 W. Walnut Street; tel: 626-577 1660; www.pasadena history.org; tours Fri–Sun at 12.15pm), now part of the Pasadena museum of history. Built in 1905, it contains the mansion's original furniture and artwork, as well as historical exhibits.

PASADENA MUSEUMS

Some of LA's finest art museums are located in Pasadena. Several lie along Colorado Boulevard.

The highly reputable **Norton Simon Museum** (411 W. Colorado Boulevard; tel: 626-449 6840; www.nortonsimon. org; Mon, Wed–Thu noon–5pm, Fri–Sat 11am–8pm, Sun 11am–5pm; free 1st Fri of each month 5–8pm) is considered to have one of the world's finest European art collections, with masterpieces by Rembrandt, Goya, Picasso, and the Impressionists. In addition, there is an extensive collection of Degas sculptures, as well as works by Rodin. An outstanding selection of sculpture from India and Southeast Asia spanning a period of 2,000 years is a perfect complement to the Western art.

The **Pacific Asia Museum** (46 North Los Robles Avenue; tel: 626-449 2742; www.pacificasiamuseum.org; Wed–Sun 10am–6pm; free 2nd Sun of each month) has been designed to resemble a Chinese imperial residence. It houses galleries of traditional and contemporary Asian art as well as a Chinese courtyard garden.

Nearby is the latest addition to the city's art scene. The **Pasadena Museum of California Art** (490 E. Union Street; tel: 626-568 3665; www.pmcaonline.org; Wed–Sun noon–5pm, 3rd Thu also 5–8pm; free 1st Fri all day and 3rd Thu 5–8pm of each month) focuses on the state's artists and their works.

PASADENA AREA'S TREASURES

Pasadena is famous for the **Rose Bowl** stadium (Rose Bowl
Drive; tel: 626-577 3100; www.rosebowlstadium.com), where,
at full capacity, 103,000 spectators watch the annual college
football game on New Year's Day. Prior to the game, one million people line Colorado Boulevard to see the **Tournament
of Roses Parade** (www.tournamentofroses.com). The stadium also hosts the 'swapmeet,' or flea market, on the second Sunday of each month (9am–4.30pm, no admittance
after 3pm). The headquarters for Pasadena's biggest event
are located in **Tournament House**, previously the **Wrigley
Mansion** (391 S. Orange Grove Boulevard; tel: 626-449 4100;
tours Feb–Aug Thu at 2pm and 4pm; free). You can tour the
former home of the chewing gum king to see its richly pan-
eled rooms, marble staircases, and ornate ceilings.

Nearby San Marino is home to a few of the county's best
museums. The **Huntington Library, Art Collections, and
Botanical Gardens** (1151 Oxford Road, San Marino; tel:
626-405 2100; www.huntington.org; late May–early Sept
Wed–Mon 10.30am–4.30pm, Sept–May Mon, Wed–Fri noon–
4.30pm, Sat–Sun 10.30am–4.30pm; free 1st Thu of every
month with advanced tickets) comprise a 207-acre (84-hec-
tare) estate owned by railroad tycoon Henry E. Huntington.
Its library is one of the most complete research facilities
in the world. Among the rarities are a Gutenberg Bible
and the illustrated Ellesmere manuscript of Chaucer's
Canterbury Tales.

The three art galleries contain one of the most comprehensive collections of British and French 18th- and 19th-
century art in the United States. Gainsborough's *Blue Boy*
and Lawrence's *Pinkie* are the showpieces of the Huntington
Gallery. In the Virginia Steele Scott Gallery you can view
American paintings from the 1730s to 1930s, while the

Arabella Huntington Collection has Renaissance paintings and 18th-century French decorative arts.

The lovely Botanical Gardens offer 130 acres (50 hectares) of changing landscapes. Among the highlights are the Desert Garden, with a vast maze of mature cacti; the Japanese garden, with ponds, fish, and drum bridge; the sweet-smelling Rose Garden, showing the history and development of the rose over 2,000 years; and the new Chinese garden.

THE SOUTH COAST

PALOS VERDES TO SAN PEDRO

The coastal bluffs of the **Palos Verdes** peninsula offer some of the loveliest views of the ocean – best enjoyed from winding Palos Verdes Drive, which hugs the coast just south of Redondo Beach. The **Point Vicente Lighthouse** (31550 Palos

Point Vicente Lighthouse

Verdes Drive; www.vicentelight.org; closed for maintenance at the time of writing), with its adjacent Interpretive Center (daily 10am–5pm, summer longer hours), is a good place to stop and stretch your legs and admire the rugged beauty of the region. It's also a prime spot for whale-watching during the winter migrations, a popular activity for tourists and locals alike.

You'll find the pretty **Wayfarer's Chapel** (5755 Palos Verdes Drive South; www.wayfarerschapel.org) on the top of the southern cliffs. This intriguing glass structure nestled amidst the trees was created by architect Frank Lloyd Wright's son as a memorial to the Swedish philosopher Emanuel Swedenborg. It is open daily for meditation.

Amid a bevy of beach towns is **San Pedro**, a working seaport that borders Los Angeles Harbor. The shipyards, stretching for miles, are most impressive from the top of the soaring arch of the Vincent Thomas Bridge. You can watch the giant cranes as they unload the cargo ships.

An attractive waterfront promenade at San Pedro offers recreational boating, whale-watching and harbor cruises. Also along the shore is the **Cabrillo Marine Aquarium** (3720 Stephen White Drive; tel: 310-548 7562; www.cabrilloaq. org; Tue–Fri noon–5pm, Sat–Sun 10am–5pm; donation suggested). Housed in a building designed by Frank Gehry, it focuses on local sea life, and contains a touch tank where kids can pet sea creatures.

LONG BEACH

Long Beach established itself as a premier seaside resort by the early 1900s. Visitors took the old electric Red Car trolley from Los Angeles to spend a day at the beach, while silent film stars built lavish summer homes on the bluffs overlooking the Pacific. Long Beach's rebirth as a tourist destination started in 1967 when the city purchased the former luxury liner, the **Queen Mary**  (1126 Queens Highway; tel: 877-342 0738; www.queen mary.com; daily 10am–6pm). The world's largest cruise ship was docked in the harbor and converted into a hotel and tourist attraction. You can wander around the grand staterooms, promenade deck, bridge, and other exhibits that portray life in the working and living quarters of the ship. The ship is purportedly haunted; if you're not afraid of spirits, book a stay overnight and explore the ship's paranormal activity on a ghost tour. There are

The Queen Mary at Long Beach

plans to create a maritime museum aboard the ship.

Looking across the harbor from the ship, you'll see Wyland's **Planet Ocean**, a 10-story mural on the 16,000 sq ft (1,485 sq m) exterior wall of the Long Beach Arena depicting whales, dolphins, and sea lions. Long Beach has some 50 murals, many dating from the 1930s. Beside it is the Long Beach Convention and Entertainment Center.

The seven-block Promenade walkway (near Pine and Long Beach Boulevard and First and Third Streets) that leads from the business district to the marina is the heart of the city's revived downtown area, with new restaurants and jazz and comedy clubs.

A top Long Beach attraction is the **Aquarium of the Pacific** ㊱ (100 Aquarium Way; tel: 562-590 3100; www.aquariumofpacific.

org; daily 9am–6pm). With nearly 500 species, it is one of the largest aquariums in the country. Exhibits focusing on three Pacific Ocean regions range from sea lions to tropical fish to the shark lagoon. There is also an aviary full of Australian parrots.

The **Long Beach Museum of Art** (2300 E. Ocean Boulevard; tel: 562-439 2119; www.lbma.org; Thu 11am–8pm, Fri–Sun 11am–5pm; free every Fri) is housed in a historic 1912 house perched on a bluff overlooking the Pacific and Long Beach harbor. Its splendid ocean views compete with the changing exhibitions of contemporary California art.

The **Museum of Latin American Art** (628 Alamitos Avenue; tel: 562-437 1689; www.molaa.com; Wed–Sun 11am–5pm, Fri until 9pm; free every Sun and 4th Fri of each month 5–9pm) occupies a former roller-skating rink in the East Village Arts District. It has contemporary works from its permanent collection as well as temporary exhibitions.

With several miles of sandy beach, Long Beach is an excellent water-sports center (see page 92). Gondola Getaway (5437 East Ocean Boulevard; tel: 562-433 9595; www.gondola getawayinc.com) offers gondola cruises through the canals of Naples Island. The restaurant and gift shop complex at Shoreline Village is an attractive remake of a typical New England harbor town.

EXCURSIONS

With a car, you are no more than a couple of hours from deserts, beaches, mountains, and any number of outstanding southern California attractions. Here are some of the key sites a short distance from Los Angeles for that special day trip.

ORANGE COUNTY

Orange County adjoins Los Angeles County to the south, but it has developed an altogether different identity. In fact, some

Angelenos refer to the county as being 'behind the orange curtain,' due to its conservative lifestyle. Along with its 42 miles (67km) of sandy beaches and beach communities, it is best known as the home of two theme parks – Disneyland and Knott's Berry Farm – and one of the nation's top convention sites. The Anaheim Visitor and Convention Bureau has lots of information on the area (see page 131).

DISNEYLAND

Since 1955, when Walt Disney opened the doors of his Magic Kingdom, **Disneyland** ㊲ (1313 S. Harbor Boulevard, Anaheim; tel: 714-781 4565; www.disneyland.com; daily, hours vary by season) has become one of the world's most popular tourist attractions. The magic of Disney comes to life in its themed 'lands,' each of which offers rides and other entertainments. **Adventureland** recreates the exotic areas of Africa and the South Pacific on its Jungle Cruise. Here, you can try out one of Disneyland's best rides, the Indiana Jones Adventure, based on Steven Spielberg's popular films. **New Orleans Square** has two of the best attractions, Pirates of the Caribbean and the Haunted Mansion. At the backwoods

The Sleeping Beauty Castle, Disneyland

setting of **Critter Country** you'll find the exciting Splash Mountain log flume ride, while **Frontierland** takes you to the realm of the pioneers, along with steamships and runaway mine trains.

Fantasyland, entered via Sleeping Beauty's castle, is pure storybook enchantment. Don't miss *It's a Small World*, everyone's favorite cruise around the globe, and **Mickey's Toontown**, a cartoon world where children can explore Mickey Mouse's neighborhood. **Tomorrowland's** futuristic world of rocket jets, Star Tours, and Space Mountain (a terrifying roller-coaster ride in the dark) has been enhanced with such items as the Michael Jackson 3-D musical *Captain EO*.

The park's finest attractions, however, begin after dark. **Main Street's** parades are filled with magnificent floats and appearances by Disney characters. Later, Tinkerbell soars above the castle to ignite a splendid fireworks display. The most fantastic show of all is Fantasmic!, an interaction of special effects, animation, and performers. The unique technology projects film images onto giant water-mist screens that are 30ft (9m) tall and 50ft (15m) wide.

Disney California Adventure Park is a separate, adjacent 55-acre (22-hectare) theme park, celebrating the state in microcosm. Here you can try your hand at animation or be a TV star; 'hang-glide' over fabulous desert landscapes; sample wines, tortillas, and sourdough; visit the Muppets or a boardwalk; and ride a looping roller-coaster or thrilling river rapids.

Long lines

Disneyland can be crowded in summer. Expect waits of 30–90 minutes for popular attractions, and heavy crowds on Main Street two hours before the parade. During high season, arrive when the park opens and hit the popular attractions before lines get too long.

KNOTT'S BERRY FARM

The nation's oldest theme park, **Knott's Berry Farm** ㉚, started as a berry farm on 20 acres (8 hectares) of rented land along a dusty road in Buena Park, just west of Anaheim (8039 Beach Boulevard, Buena Park; tel: 714-220 5200; www.knotts. com; daily, hours vary by season). In the 1930s Walter Knott began growing a new strain of berry, the boysenberry, and it soon became a booming enterprise. His wife, Cordelia, saw an opportunity to boost the family income and began serving chicken dinners on her wedding china. Soon people waited for several hours for her delicious dinners and boysenberry pies. Walter had a keen interest in the old West and, in order to create a diversion for the ravenous patrons, began building a ghost town. Many of its buildings were brought piece by piece from abandoned desert towns. Eventually, a theme park was born.

White-knuckle ride at Knott's Berry Farm

Today the original park has expanded to several themed areas in an attempt to attract audiences of all ages and interests. The Ghost Town features a GhostRider roller coaster. The highlight of Wild Water Wilderness is Bigfoot Rapids, a whitewater river ride, while Indian Trails explores Native American legends, music, and dance. Fiesta Village is a tribute to California's early Spanish heritage, with The Jaguar!

(a roller coaster) and a very rare turn-of-the-20th-century Dentzel carousel with hand-carved animals. The Boardwalk, a re-creation of a California amusement park from the 1920s, features a buffalo nickel arcade. Camp Snoopy, home of the 'Peanuts' cartoon characters, has amusements for young children. There are also thrill rides for the older crowd, including 4D interactive rides. Entertainment, from music to old-time melodrama, is offered all around the park, and Mrs Knott's chicken dinners remain in great demand.

ATTRACTIONS NEAR ANAHEIM

If you decide to skip the chicken dinner come suppertime, you can join the crowds of families at nearby Medieval Times Dinner and Tournament (7662 Beach Boulevard; http://medievaltimes.com; see page 114), where diners eat with their hands in a castle-like dining room while actors fight with swords, joust, and do all they can to amuse.

Anaheim's **GardenWalk** (321 W. Katella Avenue; www.anaheimgardenwalk.com; daily 11am–9pm) is an outdoor shopping and dining center a few minutes' away from Disneyland Resort and the Anaheim Convention Center. Themed restaurants, movie theaters and a bowling and entertainment center are set amid manicured gardens.

At the **Richard Nixon Library and Museum** (18001 Yorba Linda Boulevard, Yorba Linda; tel: 714-993 5075; www.nixonlibrary.org; Mon–Sat 10am–5pm, Sun 11am–5pm), the life of the 37th president of the United States is showcased in detail. Displays allow you to listen to a Watergate tape or 'interview' Nixon.

The **Crystal Cathedral** (12141 Lewis Street, Garden Grove; tel: 714-620 7916; www.christcathedralcalifornia. org; campus tours Mon–Fri 10am–3pm and Sat 9am–4pm; free) is a monument to its time, built over the past quarter century by television evangelist Robert Schuller. This majestic structure is something like a four-pointed star, with 10,000 panes of glass forming translucent walls supported by a steel truss frame. Following the bankruptcy of Schuller's church, the cathedral was bought by the Roman Catholic Diocese of Orange in 2011 and at the time of writing was awaiting its reopening in 2016 as the Christ Cathedral.

Crystal Cathedral

The **Bowers Museum of Cultural Art** (2002 N. Main Street, Santa Ana; tel: 714-567 3600; www.bowers.org; Tue–Sun 10am–4pm) is another local gem. Displays focus on the discovery of cultures from around the world. Permanent exhibits include pre-Columbian art.

COASTAL ORANGE COUNTY

The coastline south of Los Angeles is the ultimate California dream: the beach is always a few steps away, the pace is slower, and dress is more casual. It's the kind of place where the big decision of the day will be where you go for sunset cocktails. Life is all about the beach here, but for those antsy for action there are also some worthwhile attractions on the side and even some 'high' culture performance venues.

Lying to the north of Huntington Beach is the **Bolsa Chica Conservancy**, a salt marsh that harbors more than 300 types

Laguna Beach

of birds, which you can see along a 1.5-mile (2.5km) loop trail (3842 Warner Avenue at PCH; tel: 714-846 1114; www. bolsachica.org; daily sunrise–sunset, interpretive center daily 9am–4pm; free).

Internationally known as Surf City, **Huntington Beach** has the largest stretch of uninterrupted beachfront on the West Coast (8 miles/13km). The focal point is the famous pier, which stretches more than 1,800ft (550m) into the Pacific, and provides a great vantage point for watching surfers in action.

Newport Beach, a fashionable beach community that surrounds Newport Harbor, hosts the upscale (and aptly named) Fashion Island shopping mall (www.shopfashionisland.com). Thousands of small boats are docked here, and on weekdays the dory fishermen still sell the morning catch on the beach at Newport Pier.

Separating the marina from the ocean is pretty **Balboa Peninsula**, where a paved walkway runs in front of beach-front homes. At the southern end of the marina is the

Victorian-style Balboa Pavilion; built as a bathhouse in 1902, it hosted big-band dances in the 1940s. It is now the center of a small arcade and shopping/dining area. Harbor cruises depart from here.

Here, too, is the **Orange County Museum of Art** (850 San Clemente Drive, Newport Beach; tel: 949-759 1122; www.ocma. net; Wed–Sun 11am–5pm, Fri11am–8pm; free every Fri). Its well-regarded collection of modern and contemporary works by California-based artists ranges from Impressionism to Pop Art.

Laguna Beach is one of the coast's most attractive towns. Its history as an artists' colony in the 1950s and 1960s earned it the nickname 'SoHo by the Sea,' but, as usual, wealthy types follow hard on the heels of the artists, and today the beach is surrounded by fabulous homes perched along the hillsides and canyons. Its most famous arts festival is the **Pageant of the Masters** (www.foapom.com) in which local models enact striking tableaux of classic and modern paintings. The **Laguna Art Museum** (307 Cliff Drive; tel: 949-494 8971; www.laguna artmuseum.org; Fri–Tue 11am–5pm, Thu 11am–9pm; free 1st Thu of each month 5–9pm, see www.firstthursdaysartwalk. com) features changing exhibitions on California artists.

Mission San Juan Capistrano (tel: 949-234 1300; www. missionsjc.com; daily 9am–5pm), founded in 1776, lies inland near Dana Point, off the Ortega Highway. Although the Great Stone Church that earned it the nickname 'Jewel of the Missions' was destroyed in an earthquake in 1812 (just six years after it was completed), the beautiful grounds and adobe buildings have been restored. The Serra Chapel is the oldest building still in use in California, and the only remaining chapel where Father Junípero Serra, founder of the mission chain, celebrated Mass. The spot is perhaps best known, in legend and song, for the cliff swallows that return every spring on St Joseph's Day.

CATALINA ISLAND

One of the most popular excursions for both Angelenos and tourists is a trip to **Catalina Island**, the most developed of California's eight Channel Islands. Thousands of daytrippers come here each year to enjoy its beaches and water sports; there are also hotels for longer stays. It is easily reached by ferry from San Pedro or Long Beach, or the Catalina Flyer catamaran from Newport Beach. A helicopter service also runs to the island. Advance reservations should be made in summer.

The island's only town, **Avalon**, sits around the bay below stunning mountains that separate it from the rugged interior. Since no cars are allowed on the island, Avalon has the feel of an old-fashioned beach community. The beautiful landmark **Casino** building stands at one end of the harbor. It was built in 1929 by William Wrigley, the chewing gum magnate. For the next two decades boatloads of people came from San Pedro

Boats moored in the bay at Avalon on Catalina Island

to dance all night in the grand ballroom with its huge circular dance floor.

A number of boat trips leave from the pleasure pier. These include coastal cruises and a glass-bottomed boat trip to view the colorful fish and marine plant life. Catalina Island is a good location for scuba diving and snorkeling. The Wrigley Memorial and Botanical Garden is 2 miles (3km) inland. Most of Catalina's rugged interior is owned by the Santa Catalina Island Conservancy (www.catalinaconservancy.org), a nonprofit foundation that preserves the island's natural resources. A herd of buffalo brought here during the filming of a movie in 1924 now numbers around 150–200. Permits must be acquired for hiking or camping, but you can see the interior on an inland motor tour. The views climbing up the steep, narrow road are breathtaking.

LAKES, MOUNTAINS, AND DESERT

Los Angeles' closest mountain retreats are **Big Bear Lake** and **Lake Arrowhead**, which lie east of the city less than two hours away. They are connected by Rim of the World Drive, a scenic highway reaching elevations of 8,000ft (2,440m). These resorts are a welcome escape from the heat of the city in summer and offer many activities. In the winter, of course, Big Bear is an excellent downhill skiing area.

A fashionable way to experience the desert is by visiting one of the resort communities around **Palm Springs**, about two hours' drive east of LA. A haven for film stars and golf pros since the 1930s, it caters to a broad spectrum of visitors. You can relax at the pools or tennis courts, explore the desert landscape, take the aerial tramway for a view of sand and hills for miles, and dine at any number of fashionable restaurants. Palm Springs forms a major winter retreat for Angelenos as well as for visitors from the East Coast, but it is less popular in July and August, when temperatures soar well over 100°F (38°C).

WHAT TO DO

SHOPPING

If there was ever a shopping heaven, this is it. Everything you could possibly want is at your disposal with a flash of the credit card. With hundreds of shops located along charming streets, stacked in mega-malls, and tucked into nondescript neighborhood nooks, there's no doubt you'll find more than a few mementos to carry home.

SHOPPING DISTRICTS

Rodeo Drive in Beverly Hills is the first stop on every shopper's circuit (www.rodeodrive-bh.com). It's home to the pricey emporia Tiffany, Chanel, Louis Vuitton, and Giorgio Armani, but more affordable retailers such as Ralph Lauren and Guess vie for tourist dollars.

Funky and youthful attire is offered at every doorstep along **Melrose Avenue** between La Brea and Fairfax. Once the epi-center of hip Hollywood counterculture, this strip has become a strolling street for young tourists. Still, there are plenty of bargains to be found. Melrose Avenue carries on into West Hollywood, where, amid the art galleries and design show-rooms, you'll find exorbitantly expensive Fred Segal, the best and most celebrity-frequented mini-department store in town. Another favorite is elite clothing store Maxfield (www.maxfieldla.com), which carries a range of top designers.

Third Street, between La Cienega and Fairfax, is the Melrose alternative, with a hipper and more stylish feel, along with antiques, clothing, shoe, and gift stores. Meanwhile, **La Brea** (the blocks between Wilshire and Melrose) and **Beverly Boulevard** (between La Brea and Stanley) are for the stylish locals too old for Melrose fashion and too hip for Rodeo. Along

The elusive Rodeo Drive

both streets are retro furnishings, vintage clothing, designer boutiques, and fun gift stores. **Robertson Boulevard** (between Beverly Boulevard and Third Street; www.robertsonboulevard-shop.com) is the best place to spot celebs as they dash into trendy boutiques like Kitson. Sunset Boulevard's **Sunset Plaza** (www.sunsetplaza.com) is another stretch of hip upmarket boutiques and Hollywood culture at its most flaunting and tawdry.

The city also has more than a dozen specialized **book-shops**, including the Bodhi Tree on Melrose (www.bodhitree.com), which carries metaphysical and New Age titles, and Book Soup on Sunset Boulevard (www.booksoup.com), which also carries international newspapers and periodicals.

The Grove shopping area

Since **Santa Monica** residents wouldn't think of driving so far east to spend their money, this chic seaside town has its own selection of comparable shopping streets. Very cool **Main Street** celebrates everything from thrift shops to chic boutiques. **Montana Avenue** (https://montanaave.com) is known for pricey upscale designer apparel and furnishings. The eternally crowded **Third Street Promenade** (www.downtownsm.com) caters to both tourist and local markets with an enormous choice of affordable chain clothing stores, jewelry shops, and gift boutiques.

Over the mountains to the northeast, **Old Town Pasadena** is a lovely place to browse the enticing clothing, lingerie, and gift stores. Just north of Los Angeles, the San Fernando Valley's main drag, **Ventura Boulevard**, is the place valley-dwellers go to buy virtually everything.

CityWalk

Universal Studios' CityWalk has a wide range of retail wonders, including magic shops, toy stores, and science-fiction memorabilia.

SHOPPING MALLS

In a town where time in traffic is to be avoided at all costs, one-stop shopping is essential. In shopping malls, everything you're looking for is available without moving your car. The Beverly Hills set usually bops over to **Westfield Century City** (www.westfield.com/centurycity), a pleasant open-air mall with a stadium-seating movie theater. Bordering West Hollywood and Beverly Hills is the 200-plus store **Beverly Center** (www.beverlycenter.com); Westwood has the **Westside Pavilion** (www.westsidepavilion.com); while in the Fairfax District the Farmers' Market has expanded into **The Grove** (www.thegrovela.com), a smart outdoor shopping area with upmarket chain stores. By the sea, head for **Santa Monica Place** mall (www.santamonicaplace.com) at the end of the Third Street Promenade.

On the periphery, there's the Valley's **Sherman Oaks Galleria** (www.shermanoaksgalleria.com) and nearby **Fashion Square** (www.westfield.com/fashionsquare). Orange County residents rejoice over Costa Mesa's **South Coast Plaza** (www.southcoastplaza.com), their classiest and most extensive mall with 300 stores, including designer outlets. **Fashion Island** (www.shopfashionisland.com) in Newport Beach is another good shopping enclave.

Department stores such as Macy's, Nordstrom, Bloomingdale's, Neiman-Marcus, Saks Fifth Avenue, and Barneys New York (the latter three with valet parking) are strategically located around town, often in more than one location. Many can be found along Wilshire Boulevard in Beverly Hills.

BARGAINS

LA's **Fashion District** (http://fashiondistrict.org) is the hub of the West Coast garment industry. It covers 90 blocks southeast of central Downtown, spreading out from a hub around Los Angeles and 11th streets. Most of the designer showrooms are wholesale businesses, but there are also hundreds of retail shops which sell discounted clothing and accessories. On Saturdays many wholesale-only stores sell to the general public. The **Jewelry District** (http://the-jewelry-district.com) is also situated on nearby Hill Street, between West Fifth and West Sixth streets.

Flea markets – usually called swap meets – sell antiques, old Levi's, and every kind of vintage treasure you could imagine.

OUTDOOR MARKETS

Strolling the city's open-air markets is an excellent way to grab some delicious and inexpensive grub and mingle with the locals. The famous Farmers Market at Third and Fairfax is a mixture of old folks, tourists, and hip Hollywood types who crowd the excellent food stands. Santa Monica's outdoor farmers' market is held Wednesday and Saturday 8.30am–1pm along Arizona Avenue at the Third Street Promenade. Smaller farmer's markets are held on every day of the week in different locations throughout the city.

Downtown's Grand Central Market on Broadway is LA's oldest and largest open-air produce market. Also Downtown is the Flower Market, on Wall and 8th streets; the best selections are found before dawn.

They're held throughout the city, but an in-town favorite is the Melrose Trading Post held every Sunday 9am–5pm at Fairfax High School. One of the best is on the second Sunday of every month from 9am to 3pm at the Rose Bowl in Pasadena.

SPORTS

SPECTATOR SPORTS

You can experience America's *An LA farmers' market* favorite summer pastime by grabbing a hot dog and a beer and rooting for the Dodgers baseball team at **Dodger Stadium** (1000 Elysian Park Avenue; tel: 866-800 1275; www.dodgers.com), just north of Downtown in Chavez Ravine. In Anaheim you can cheer on the Angels at **Angel Stadium** (2000 Gene Autry Way, Anaheim; tel: 714-940 2000; www.angelsbaseball.com).

From October to April it's basketball season, when both the Lakers and the Clippers run the court at the Downtown **Staples Center** (1111 S. Figueroa Street; tel: 213-742 7100; www.staples center.com). College football games, played from August to December, are as entertaining as NFL and AFL games. UCLA plays at the **Rose Bowl** (see page 70), while USC games are at the **Los Angeles Memorial Coliseum** (3939 S. Figueroa Street; tel: 213-747 7111; www.lacoliseum.com). Ice hockey fans can watch the Los Angeles Kings play at the Staples Center (from November to March); Anaheim's Ducks play at the **Honda Center** (2695 E. Katella Avenue; tel: 714-704 2500; www.honda center.com) of Anaheim, across from Anaheim Stadium.

The **Toyota Grand Prix** auto race is held in Long Beach (www.gplb.com) every April. The **Northern Trust Open** finds world-class golf champions flocking to the city each February for the tournament at the Riviera Country Club, Pacific Palisades (www.northerntrustopen.com).

Santa Anita Park (285 W. Huntington Drive; tel: 626-574 7223; www.santaanita.com) in Arcadia offers two horse-racing seasons: fall and winter/spring. While **Hollywood Park Racetrack** in Inglewood was demolished in 2015 to make space for the 80,000-seat City of Champions Stadium scheduled for 2018, the Hollywood Park Casino remains a simulcast wagering facility (1050 S. Prairie Avenue; tel: 310-330-3514; www.hollywoodpark. com). **Los Alamitos** racecourse (4961 Katella Avenue; tel: 714-820 2800; www.losalamitos.com), near Disneyland, has quarterhorse racing and thoroughbred racing throughout the year.

With several yacht clubs based in Long Beach, the city hosts races, regattas and other yachting competitions.

OUTDOOR ACTIVITIES AND OTHER SPORTS

With exceptional year-round weather, over 72 miles (116km) of beaches, vast mountain ranges, and a hyperathletic community, Los Angeles has enough outdoor activities to keep you busy for the next 10 years.

Seaside fun is yours if you hit the coastal bike, skate, and jogging paths (for maps and guides, call the Visitor Information Line (tel: 310-305 9545) or stop off at the **Marina del Rey** Visitor Information Center (4701 Admiralty Way, Marina del Rey; www.visitmarinadelrey.com). The Los Angeles segment of the **Pacific Coast Bicentennial Bike Route** is a popular trail. For information and maps of LA bike routes, Los Angeles Bike Paths has a useful website, www.labikepaths.com.

More than 100 **golf courses** are open to the public. The City of Los Angeles operates seven 18-hole and five 9-hole courses; for information on these courses and reservations call 818-291 9980, or visit www.golf.lacity.org. Public courses are popular, so book in advance.

For information on **tennis** and other sports, see the LA Department of Recreation and Parks website at laparks. org or tel: 818-291 9980.Golf and tennis are also available in Orange County and in the desert communities in and around Palm Springs.

Hiking trails abound in the Santa Monica and San Gabriel mountains. For information on local hiking trails, contact the **Angeles National Forest** (tel: 626-574 1613; www.fs.usda. gov/angeles). For a closer spot to check out nature, visit **Griffith Park** or **Franklin Canyon**. The best place to jog is the **Hollywood Reservoir** in the Hollywood Hills.

For hiking in Pasadena's **Eaton Canyon** call the Nature Center (tel: 626-398 5420; www.ecnca.org). A series of

The Los Angeles area is ideal for cyclists

self-guided nature trails and some longer hiking trails wind through **Will Rogers State Historic Park** in the Pacific Palisades (tel: 310-454 8212; www.parks.ca.gov/willrogers, see page 51). Lake Arrowhead and Big Bear Lake, about two hours' drive east in the **San Bernardino National Forest** (www. fs.usda.gov/sbnf), consist of rugged mountain terrain. Contact either of the tourist offices in theseareas (see page 131).

For information about parks and activities in the Santa Monica Mountains, call the Visitor Center at tel: 805-370 2301 or head-quarters at tel: 805-370 2300 (www.nps.gov/samo). The **National Park Service** (www.nps.gov) can also give information about facilities and events in the West Coast's national park system.

Horseback riding is popular in the Los Angeles area. Diamond Bar Stables (tel: 818-242 8443; www.rockenpoutfitters.com) and the LA Equestrian Center (tel: 818-840 9063; www.la-equestrian center.com) use good bridle trails.

WATER SPORTS AND ACTIVITIES

The Pacific coast from Santa Barbara south through Orange County is one big water playground. Beaches from Long Beach to Malibu are perfect for surfing, boogie-boarding, wading, and swimming. Beachfront sports shops are willing to rent you a board and can usually direct you toward lessons as well.

Meanwhile, Long Beach is a major center for **boating**; you can rent sailboats, dinghies, canoes, and powerboats of all sizes. Marina del Rey is another, where you can also charter a yacht. In Orange County, Newport Beach is a major center for rentals, and so is Dana Point to the south. If you are hap-pier to leave the seamanship to someone else, take a harbor cruise at Marina del Rey, San Pedro, or the Balboa Peninsula. For a more romantic outing, try a gondola at Naples, near Long Beach. **Whale-watching** expeditions are organized during the winter migrations; they leave from Marina del Rey, San Pedro,

Newport Beach, and Long Beach. Jet skis can be rented in the above towns as well as in Malibu. Try parasailing at the Balboa Pavilion. You can rent kayaking or windsurfing equipment in Long Beach, Malibu, and Marina del Rey.

Other popular water sports include **scuba diving** and **snorkeling**. One of the best places to see underwater marine life is at Catalina Island, but equipment rental is also available in Long Beach, Redondo Beach, and Malibu. The best spot in Orange County is Laguna Beach, as the entire city beach area is a designated marine preserve.

Surfing at Zuma Beach, Malibu

WINTER SPORTS

Nearby mountain ranges make downhill skiing a popular winter sport. Further east is **Mt Baldy** (tel: 909-982 0800; www.mtbaldy skilifts.com). Ski areas usually sell out on weekends, and visitors are advised to buy lift tickets in advance by calling the resort directly. Larger ski resorts are under two hours away. The most popular is **Big Bear**. For information contact the Big Bear Lake Resort Association (tel: 800-424 4232; www.bigbearinfo.com).

ENTERTAINMENT

The entertainment capital of the world sure knows how to entertain. There are jazz clubs, world-class opera and symphony performances, comedy clubs, Broadway shows, concerts, strip clubs, transvestite reviews, and swing, country-western, and salsa clubs. You name it – LA's got it. To find out what's going on, pick up any of the city's free weekly papers (see page 125).

THE ARTS

LA's concert halls and theaters present some of the best music and drama in the country. The city's premier venue is Downtown's **Music Center** (tel: 213-972 7211; www.music center.org). It has several components: the **Dorothy Chandler Pavilion** presents classical music, opera, and ballet; the **Ahmanson Theater** hosts big musicals; and the **Mark Taper Forum** offers a more intimate setting for contemporary drama. The **Walt Disney Concert Hall** is the home of the Los Angeles Philharmonic and Los Angeles Master Chorale.

The **Geffen Playhouse** (10886 Le Conte Avenue, Westwood; tel: 310-208 5454; www.geffenplayhouse.com) stages musicals and comedies. The **Dolby Theatre**, formerly the Kodak Theatre, in Hollywood (6801 Hollywood Boulevard; tel: 323-308 6300; www.dolbytheatre.com) hosts music concerts and ballets. Visiting dance groups and bands perform at the **Shrine Auditorium** in downtown LA (665 W. Jefferson Boulevard; tel: 213-748 5116; www.shrineauditorium.com) and at the Center for the Art of Performance **at UCLA's Royce Hall** (340 Royce Drive, Westwood; http://cap.ucla.edu).

Opposite the Staples Center downtown, the new state-of-the-art **Microsoft Theatre**, formerly the NOKIA Theatre, (777 Chick Hearn Court and Figueroa Street; tel: 213-763

Tickets

Tickets to shows and concerts can be booked at the venue or by phone (with credit card) from ticket agencies such as Ticketmaster (tel: 213-480 3232; www.ticketmaster. com). For tickets to television recordings, see page 129.

6020; www.microsofttheater.com) presents concerts, performances and events on southern California's largest stage. Also downtown is the venerable **Orpheum Theatre** (842 S. Broadway, tel: 877-677 4386; www.laorpheum.com), which opened in 1926. It has played host to some of the most famous names in showbusiness and continues to present a wide range of performances.

The **Santa Monica Pier** is the coastal setting for the free summer Twilight Concert Series. Other free music and dance programs are held during the summer

Walt Disney Concert Hall

at the California Plaza **Watercourt** Downtown (www.grandperformances.org).

The **Segerstrom Center for the Arts** (600 Town Center Drive, Costa Mesa; tel: 714-556 2787; www.scfta.org) sponsors symphony, chamber music, and opera performances. The South Coast Repertory Theater is based here.

AMPHITHEATERS

Few experiences are as quintessentially southern Californian as entertainment under the stars. The **Hollywood Bowl** (2301 N. Highland Avenue; tel: 323-850 2000; www.hollywoodbowl.com), summer home of the Los Angeles Philharmonic and jazz and pop concerts by the Hollywood Bowl Orchestra, fills each

Hollywood Bowl

performance with Angelenos toting gourmet picnic baskets. The nearby **Ford Amphitheatre** (2580 Cahuenga Boulevard East; tel: 323-461 3673; www.fordamphitheater. org) is the historic setting for Shakespeare plays, summer music, and cabaret. The **Greek Theatre** (tel: 323-665 5857; www.greektheatrela. com) in Griffith Park is a favorite venue for rock and pop concerts.

FILM

Want to catch up on the hottest independent film or watch a blockbuster in the TCL Chinese Theatre (www.tclchinese theatres.com) or El Capitan (https://elcapitantheatre.com)? Just dial 323-777-FILM (3456) to find out what's playing. You might spot a celeb at the hip Arclight Cinemas on Sunset Boulevard (www.arclightcinemas.com). The Laemmle Theater chain (www.laemmle.com) shows top foreign releases. The Landmark (www.landmarktheatres.com) in West LA operates numerous state-of-the-art screens showing first-run and indie movies. The AMC Century City 15 Theaters (www. amctheatres.com) in the Westfield shopping center, the Pacific Theatres Stadium 14 at the Grove (www.pacifictheatres.com), and the AMC CityWalk Stadium 19 Cinemas next to Universal Studios are other big cinema complexes.

NIGHTLIFE

Some of the most famous **nightclubs** are found on Sunset Boulevard, including Whisky-a-Go-Go (www.whiskyagogo.

com) and The Roxy (www.theroxy.com). Another is the Troubadour (www.troubadour.com) on Santa Monica Boulevard. The hippest **bars** are scattered throughout Hollywood and western LA, including SkyBar, Bar 1200, Bar Marmont, and The Well. Good spots for **blues** are Harvelle's in Santa Monica (http://harvelles.com), and the House of Blues in West Hollywood (www.houseofblues.com/losangeles). Among the many **jazz** clubs are the famed Jazz Bakery (http://jazzbakery.org) which plans to move to a new permanent home designed by Frank Ghery next to the Kirk Douglas Theater in the heart of Culver City, the Catalina Bar and Grill in Hollywood (www.catalina jazzclub.com), and the Baked Potato in North Hollywood (www.thebakedpotato.com).

Cabaret entertainment can be found at the Center Stage Theater (http://centerstagefontana.com), which is home to Tibbies Great American Cabaret. Marty and Elayne, the husband-and-wife lounge duo performing for nearly 20 years at The Dresden in Los Feliz (www.thedresden.com), are Los Angeles legends.

Comedy clubs are big. Venues include The Comedy Store

COCKTAILS WITH A VIEW

Unless you're at the beach, there may be no better way to welcome a famous California sunset than perching yourself and a cocktail at one of the city's vista cocktail rooms.

You can watch the city light up the night from a number of unique spots: the landmark Yamashiro restaurant, the Penthouse lounge at the Huntley Santa Monica Beach, the Mondrian Hotel's SkyBar, the balcony at The Sunset Tower hotel's restaurant, or the bar in the Sky penthouse at the exclusive club Soho House (if you're lucky enough to know someone who's a member).

(http://thecomedystore.com) and The Laugh Factory (www.laughfactory.com) on Sunset Boulevard, and the Hollywood Improv (http://improv.com) on Melrose Avenue.

Coffeehouses are everywhere, many offering live entertainment and poetry readings. Some of the best are clustered in Santa Monica and in West Hollywood.

Billiards is another fun night-time option. Try Q's Billiard Club (http://qsbilliardclub.com) in Brentwood.

CHILDREN'S LOS ANGELES

This is certainly one city where you will never run out of things to do or places to go to keep the kids amused. Topping the list are the region's theme parks: Disneyland, Knott's Berry Farm, and Universal Studios. Farther away is Valencia's **Six Flags Magic Mountain** (tel: 661-255 4100; www.sixflags.com/magicmountain), renowned for high-speed roller coasters, and **Raging Waters** (tel: 909-802 2200; www.ragingwaters.com) in San Dimas, a fun water park.

Kidspace Children's Museum (tel: 626-449 9144; www.kidspacemuseum.org) in Pasadena lets kids direct TV shows and don astronaut outfits (up to age 12). The excellent **Natural History Museum** of Los Angeles County (see page 61) and its Burbank branch are great for the whole family. The highly rated **California Science Center and IMAX Theater** (see page 62) has interactive exhibits. The **La Brea Tar Pits Museum** is a local favorite.

The Los Angeles Zoo (see page 63) is in Griffith Park, and other attractions in Griffith Park include train, pony, and stagecoach rides, and a carousel. **Santa Monica Pier** is fun-filled with a carousel and other rides, arcade games, and inexpensive carnival food.

There's no better way to wear out kids than a day at the well-equipped beaches.

CALENDAR OF EVENTS

Whatever the time of year, there'll be a party somewhere in LA.

January Tournament of Roses Parade (Rose Bowl Parade), Pasadena, New Year's Day.

January/February Chinese New Year Celebration, Chinatown.

March Fiesta de las Golondrinas (Return of the Swallows) – month-long festivities at Mission San Juan Capistrano, St Joseph's Day March 19.

April Los Angeles Times Festival of Books, the largest book festival in the country.

May Cinco de Mayo, Mexican Independence Day, Olvera Street. Venice Art Walk – open studios, galleries, and homes in Venice artists' colony. The music and entertainment festival WorldFest has transformed itself into the VegFest, commencing in 2016.

June Playboy Jazz Festival, Hollywood Bowl. Los Angeles Pride – two-day LGBT festival with parade, West Hollywood. Los Angeles Film Festival – over 10 days in Westwood Village and other venues. Mariachi USA Festival – Latin music at the Hollywood Bowl.

July Orange County Fair, Costa Mesa. Pageant of the Masters live models re-create classical works of art, Laguna Canyon, through August, plus the Sawdust Art Festival across the road through August.

August Long Beach Jazz Festival – three days of world-class jazz overlooking the marina. Los Angeles African Marketplace and Cultural Faire – over three weekends, downtown LA. Nisei Week Japanese Festival, Little Tokyo.

September LA County Fair, County Fair & Exposition Center, Pomona.

October West Hollywood celebrates Halloween with the week-long Halloween Carnival ending in a wild costume party on October 31.

November Hollywood Christmas Parade – celebrities, floats, and marching bands, Sunday after Thanksgiving. Pasadena Doo-Dah Parade – spoof of the Tournament of Roses Parade.

December Light Festival – lighted displays with holiday themes at the ZOO, Griffith Park. Marina Del Rey Holiday Boat Parade – decorated brightly lit boats parade around the marina.

EATING OUT

Like its entertainment industry, LA's restaurants are often as much about image as they are about cuisine. The most popular restaurants attract a steady clientele, inspire the hip and famous to clamor for a reservation, and try to provide a special something that can't be found at the next place.

With nearly 20,000 dining options, that 'special something' comes in the form of everything from fast-food shacks to four-star formal affairs, which are invariably garnished with colorful Angelenos doing their thing. In fact, waiting for a chili dog and fries with a virtual people zoo at Pink's sidewalk grubbery is as glamorous an experience as dining alfresco next to Angelina Jolie at glitzy Spago. Wherever you dine, it's bound to be fun.

Although restaurant decor and glitz are often appetizing enough to keep diners coming back, in recent years

Dining alfresco at The Ivy

the dining experience has focused more on the food itself. With fantastic farm-fresh produce and superior fish and meats widely available throughout the state, today's 'California cuisine' reflects whatever's in season. The results are vibrant and creative preparations that are generously infused with influences from across the globe. Whether you crave sushi, French, Mexican, Burmese, Italian, vegetarian, or anything else imaginable, this town's got it and got it good.

Street food in Southern California

You can get away with spending next to nothing at ethnic eateries, or you can pay premium prices at any of the high-end haunts. But even eating at the top of the food chain doesn't have to break your budget. There's almost always something relatively affordable on the menu. If your pocketbook doesn't permit full-blown indulgence and you still want to check out one of the finer dining rooms, eat light (appetizers, salads) or consider going at lunchtime, when the prices are lower.

As for the ancillaries, desserts are decadent and splurge-worthy everywhere, which makes you wonder how everyone stays so fit. Wine lists highlight the state's best vintages.

Most areas have a range of restaurants to suit all budgets. Three of the most popular areas for dining out are West Hollywood, Beverly Hills, and Santa Monica; these are also the places where you will find the widest range of choices.

American breakfast of pancakes, bacon and eggs

Reservations are generally not required except in very prestigious or popular establishments.

BREAKFAST

In this town breakfast is not a meal – it's an event. At hotels like the Bel-Air and Four Seasons, the power breakfast has replaced the business lunch for making deals between hand-shakes and cell phone calls. Meanwhile, morning coffee culture and people-watching are at their best at the hundreds of cafés scattered from Downtown to the beaches.

As for the fare, you'll usually find everything from tradi-tional pancakes or eggs Benedict to Mexican-style *huevos rancheros* (fried eggs smothered in salsa, served on corn tortillas with a side of refried beans). Menus are always rounded out with healthier and lighter options such as fresh fruit, yogurt, and a selection of muffins, pastries, and bagels. Fresh-squeezed juices (and combinations of them, in iced 'smoothies') are a particular delight in southern California.

Practically every restaurant accommodates special off-the-menu requests.

VARIED CUISINE

LA's large ethnic populations are reflected in the wonderful diversity of the city's restaurants, with practically every kind of international cuisine available somewhere nearby.

LA's sushi is the best in the state, exquisitely presented in Japanese restaurants from Downtown to the Westside; don't forget to check out the Little Tokyo district for the atmosphere as well as the food.

Chinese restaurants specializing in regional variations – Peking, Szechwan, Shanghai, Hunan, Cantonese – range from elegant establishments in Beverly Hills to simple dining rooms in Chinatown. And if you've never had spicy Korean cuisine, there are good restaurants on every block in Koreatown.

DINING DO'S

The most popular meals to dine out in LA are arguably breakfast and lunch, when you can dine alfresco in the Southern Calforrnia sunshine. Angelenos are up early: Breakfast is served from around 6.30 until 11am, although many diners and cafés serve breakfast all day, especially on the weekends. Lunch hours are from 11.30am until 2.30pm, though hob-nobbing Hollywood types like to lunch late. Dinner is served from 5.30 until around 10.30pm, although there are plenty of late-night dining spots.

If you're going to grab a cocktail after dinner, don't forget ID: The legal drinking age in California is 21, but proof of age is frequently required for those older. Cocktail lounges and nightclubs do not admit people under the age of 21. Alcohol cannot be bought or consumed in public establishments between 2 and 6am.

Jewish delicatessens are located in many areas, especially along Fairfax Avenue and on Beverly Boulevard, where you can order up corned beef or pastrami sandwiches, matzo ball soup, cheese blintzes, as well as yummy potato pancakes.

Stalls selling Mexican food abound at Grand Central Market on Broadway or along Olvera Street, where zesty tacos, burritos, and other regional specialties are served streetside. Come nightfall, mobile taco trucks can be spotted all over the city and are a great place to grab a snack post bar-hopping. In fact, food trucks in general have become something of a craze in the city; gourmet ones now troll the streets offering everything from Korean barbecue burritos to *dim sum*, *schnitzel*, and Vietnamese sandwiches called *banh mi*.

California rolls

DRINKS

The morning, afternoon, and evening ritual of coffee-drinking takes on a humorous dimension in Los Angeles, where a java comes in enough sizes, variations, flavors, and calorific levels to confuse even the most sophisticated connoisseur. Whether you want yours with steamed milk, soy milk, vanilla, decaf espresso, or a lemon twist, all you need to do is be savvy enough to order it. An added bonus is excellent people-watching, which comes free of charge at most cafés.

Meanwhile, libations have developed a culture of their own. After the roaring 1990s, the champagne flow has slowed down a little bit but cocktails are still a popular way to toast the town. Creative concoctions boasting market-fresh ingredients have become as important to some restaurants as the dinner menu itself. Of course, the classic Mexican margarita is a local favourite made of tequila, triple sec, and (at the good establishments) fresh lime juice and simple syrup.

Celebrity hotspots

For the best shot at being seated next to someone famous, reserve a table at Mr Chow, Madeo, or The Ivy on Robertson. Or drop in for cocktails at the Four Seasons, a celebrity home-away-from-home, or the poolside Tropicana Bar at The Roosevelt Hotel, a frequent social spot for local celebs and visiting rock stars. Arrive before 8pm if you're not staying at the hotel; the guest list is often exclusive and everyone else is turned away.

At the dinner table, however, the most popular beverage is still California wine, which is showcased in virtually every dining establishment. With Napa Valley, Sonoma Valley, and, more recently, Central Coast varietals contending with France's finest, it's truly difficult to order a bad wine, whether by the glass or bottle.

The main red wines you'll find are Cabernet Sauvignon, Pinot Noir, and red Zinfandel. With whites, Chardonnay is often served as house wine, but it's become popular to experiment with Sauvignon Blancs, Pinot Grigios, and other lesser-known varietals.

Along with a good wine selection, many of LA's bars specialize in offering a wide range of local and West Coast beers and ales, though there are also English-style pubs in Santa Monica where you can find a pint of bitter.

PLACES TO EAT

As a guide, we have used the following symbols to give an indication of the price of a two-course meal for one (excluding drinks, tax, or tip), based on the average cost of main courses.

$$$$ = $50 and up $$$ = $25–$50
$$ = $$15–$25 $ = under $15

ANAHEIM

McCormick and Schmick's Grille $$–$$$ *321 West Katella Avenue, Anaheim, tel: 714-535 9000,* www.mccormickandschmicks.com. Traditional seafood restaurant that also serves steaks and fresh salads. Convenient location near Disneyland and the Anaheim Convention Center. Sun–Thu 11.30am–10pm, Fri–Sat 11.30am–11pm.

HOLLYWOOD

The Hungry Cat $$–$$$ *1535 North Vine Street, tel: 323-462 2155,* www.thehungrycat.com. An outstanding raw bar with creatively cooked seafood dishes in a sleek and modern (but lively) setting, with top-notch cocktails to boot. Mon–Wed noon–10pm, Thu–Fri noon–11pm, Sat 11am–11pm, Sun 11am–10pm.

Musso and Frank Grill $$$ *6667 Hollywood Boulevard, tel: 323-467 7788,* http://mussoandfrank.com. Hollywood's oldest restaurant (established in 1919) has dark paneling, leather booths, seasoned waiters, and great Martinis. Famous customers have included Charlie Chaplin (who sat at table no 1 in the west room), Ernest Hemingway, Raymond Chandler, Orson Welles, Humphrey Bogart, Al Pacino, and Sean Penn. American-style dishes such as steaks, chops, clams, and macaroni and cheese come à la carte. The crepe-thin pancakes are hugely popular. Tue–Sat 11am–11pm.

Providence $$$–$$$$ *5955 Melrose Avenue, tel: 323-460 4170,* www.providencela.com. Elegant restaurant with sleek, modern décor, specializing in premium wild seafood and shellfish, simply prepared and presented. Lunch Fri noon–2pm, dinner Mon–Fri 6–10pm, Sat 5.30–10pm and Sun 5.30–9pm.

MID-WILSHIRE

A.O.C. $$–$$$ *8700 West Third Street, tel: 310-859 9859,* www.aoc winebar.com. An elegant cross between a wine bar and tapas-style restaurant, with a delectable range of small plates ranging from charcuterie to oven-roasted fish and vegetables to fine cheeses, with dozens of wines by the glass. Reservations recommended. Mon 11.30am–10pm, Tue–Fri 11.30am–11pm, Sat 10am–11pm, Sun 10am–10pm.

Toast Bakery Cafe $$ *8221 West Third Street, tel: 323-655 5018,* http://toastbakerycafe.net. An excellent American menu of all-day breakfast (including a number of healthy and vegetarian options), sandwiches, pastas, other specialties, and fabulous baked goods. Daily 7.30am–6pm.

Matsuhisa $$$–$$$$ *129 North La Cienega Boulevard, Beverly Hills, tel: 310-659 9639,* www.nobumatsuhisa.com. Considered the best Asian-inspired seafood in town, chef Nobu Matsuhisa's novel menu features top-notch sushi and pages of entrées. Always crowded and noisy. Reservations necessary. Mon–Fri 11.45am–2.15pm, dinner daily 5.45–10.15pm.

WEST HOLLYWOOD

Barney's Beanery $–$$ *8447 Santa Monica Boulevard, tel: 323-654 2287,* www.barneysbeanery.com. Known for burgers, giant hot dogs, famous chili, Mexican fare, and around 200 bottled beers. Funky bar décor, pool tables, and late-night dining for LA's bar-hoppers. Mon–Fri 11am–2am, Sat–Sun 9am–2am.

Chin Chin $$ *8618 W. Sunset Boulevard (in Sunset Plaza), tel: 310-652 1818,* www.chinchin.com. Great for people-watching and relatively healthy dim sum and noodle dishes within full Chinese menu. Indoor and outdoor dining. Sun–Thu 11am–10pm, Fri–Sat 11am–11pm.

Dan Tana's $$–$$$ *9071 Santa Monica Boulevard, tel: 310-275 9444,* www.dantanasrestaurant.com. A classic old-style Hollywood restaurant with northern Italian cuisine featuring veal, chicken, seafood, and the best cut of New York steak in town. Mon–Sat 5pm–1am, Sun 5pm–12.30am.

Urth Caffe $$ *8565 Melrose Avenue, tel: 310-659 0628,* www.urth caffe.com. A popular café and casual lunch spot with organic coffee and tea. Healthy meals are on offer and there is a selection of delicious desserts which are made in house. The outdoor patio is a well-known spot for celeb-spotting. Daily 6am–11.30pm.

Pink's Famous Hot Dogs $ *709 North La Brea Avenue, tel: 323-931 4223,* www.pinkshollywood.com. The place to go when you're dying for a greasy quick bite. Hot dogs, burgers, sinful chili, and renowned fries are devoured at outdoor picnic tables. Sun–Thu 9.30am–2am, Fri–Sat 9.30am–3am. Cash only.

Versailles $–$$ *1415 South La Cienega Boulevard, tel: 310-289 0392,* www.versaillescuban.com. Locals frequent this inexpensive, delicious Cuban diner. Noteworthy garlic chicken as well as excellent pork and shrimp dishes are served in the ultra-casual dining room. Sun–Thu 11am–10pm, Fri–Sat 11am–11pm.

BEVERLY HILLS

Bouchon Bistro $$$–$$$$ *235 North Canon Drive, tel: 310-271 9910,* www.thomaskeller.com. Thomas Keller's third location of his famous restaurant packs in movie stars and foodies who come for outstanding French bistro cuisine. The adjoining bakery is a must-visit. Lunch Mon–Fri 11.30am–10.30pm, Sat 11am–10.30pm and Sun 11am–9pm.

Il Fornaio $$$ *301 North Beverly Drive, tel: 310-550 8330,* www.il fornaio.com. A bustling and bright Italian trattoria with excellent breads, soups, pizzas, pastas, and rotisserie dishes and lively, crowded atmosphere. Wood stove; mesquite grill. Patio dining. There's also a bakery café. Reservations recommended. Mon–Thu 7am–10pm, Fri 7am–11pm, Sat 7.30am–11pm, Sun 7.30am–10pm.

Lawry's Prime Rib $$$ *100 North La Cienega Boulevard, tel: 310-652 2827,* www.lawrysonline.com. A venerable temple of prime ribs, also featuring lobster, fresh fish and their dramatic and delectable 'spinning bowl' salad. Mon–Fri 5–10pm, Sat 4.30–11pm, Sun 4–9.30pm. Reservations recommended.

Mr Chow $$$–$$$$ *344 North Camden Drive, tel: 310-278 9911,* www.mrchow.com. Celebrity spotting generally accompanies excellent Beijing-style (multiple-dish) Chinese fare including duck, dumplings, lobster, and house-made garlic noodles. A modern, see-and-be-seen setting. Reservations recommended. Lunch Mon–Fri noon–2.30pm, dinner daily 6–11.30pm.

THE WESTSIDE

La Serenata Gourmet $–$$ *10924 West Pico Boulevard, tel: 310-441 9667,* www.laserenataonline.com. It's not the bare-bones atmosphere but the excellent fish, tacos, moles, enchiladas, and zesty sauces that bring crowds to this bustling Mexican restaurant. Mon–Fri 11am–3pm and 5–10pm, Fri until 11pm, Sat 11am–11pm, Sun 10am–10pm.

Father's Office $$ *3229 Helms Avenue, tel: 310-736 2224,* www.fathersoffice.com. The gourmet blue cheese burgers served at at this upscale gastropub are famous, but equally deserving are the locavore small plates and the seasonally rotating selection of 36 craft beers on tap. ID is required. Mon–Thur 5pm–11pm, Fri–Sat noon–midnight, Sun noon–10pm, bar open later.

Shaherzad Restaurant $$ *1422 Westwood Boulevard, tel: 310-470-3242,* www.shaherzadrestaurant.com. In an area known as Little Persia, this casual restaurant serves up some of the most authentic Iranian cuisine around, with grilled kabobs, savory rice dishes, and an open oven that produces freshly-baked flatbread. Daily 11.30am–11pm.

Wolfgang Puck at Hotel Bel-Air $$$–$$$$ *701 Stone Canyon Road (at Hotel Bel Air), tel: 310-909 1644,* www.dorchestercollection.com. Celebrity Chef Wolfgang Puck's delicious, creative California-

Mediterranean menu served in the glamorous dining room or on the beautiful Spanish-style terrace. Reached by crossing a bridge over a swan-filled stream and tropical gardens. Reservations necessary. Breakfast daily 7am–10.30am, lunch Mon–Sat 11.30am–2.30pm, brunch Sun 11am–3pm, dinner Sun–Thu 6–10pm, Fri–Sat 6–10.30pm, afternoon tea and all-day menu also available.

SANTA MONICA/BEACH COMMUNITIES

Border Grill $$–$$$ *1445 4th Street, Santa Monica, tel: 310-451 1655,* www.bordergrill.com. Upscale Mexican fare with a Yucatán influence and festive atmosphere. Mon–Fri 11.30am–10pm, Fri until 11pm, Sat–Sun 10am–10pm, Sat until 11pm.

Cafe del Rey $$$ *4451 Admiralty Way, Marina del Rey, tel: 310-823 6395,* www.cafedelreymarina.com. One of the area's better restaurants overlooks the marina and serves Pacific Rim 'new wave' cuisine in a modern and airy dining room. Lunch Mon–Fri 11.30am–2.30pm, dinner Mon–Thu 5.30–10pm, Fri–Sat 5.30–10.30pm, Sun 5–9.30pm; brunch Sat 11.30am–2.30pm, Sun 10.30am–2.30pm.

Chinois on Main $$$$ *2709 Main Street, Santa Monica, tel: 310-392 9025,* www.wolfgangpuck.com. Renowned chef Wolfgang Puck's chic, trendy restaurant serves a creative blend of Chinese, French, and California cuisines in a bright, loud dining room. Lunch Wed–Fri 11.30am–2pm, dinner Mon–Thu 6–10pm, Fri–Sat 6–10.30pm, Sun 5.30–10pm.

Gladstone's 4 Fish $$–$$$ *17300 Pacific Coast Highway, Pacific Palisades, tel: 310-454 3474,* http://gladstones.com. This seafood restaurant's popularity is largely due to its enormous and fun deck seating overlooking the sea. Not affiliated with the one at Universal CityWalk. Mon–Thu 11am–9pm, Fri 11am–10pm, Sat 9am–10pm, Sun 9am–9pm.

Hillstone $$$ *202 Wilshire Boulevard, tel: 310-576 7558;* www.hillstone.com. The appealing menu features prime steaks, seafood, burgers, salads as well as handcrafted sushi. In other words: this place appeals to all tastes. The warm ambience and stylish interior make for a superb experience. Sun–Tue 11.30am–10pm and Wed–Sat 11.30am–11pm.

Ivy at the Shore $$$ *1535 Ocean Avenue, Santa Monica, tel: 310-393 3113;* www.theivyrestaurants.com. Excellent California-fresh fare with a Southern accent, such as Cajun pizza or fried chicken. Especially renowned for crab cakes, grilled-vegetable salad, and healthy menu items. Daily 9.30am–10pm.

Michael's $$$–$$$$ *1147 3rd Street, Santa Monica, tel: 310-451 0843,* www.michaelssantamonica.com. One of the original examples of California cuisine and a top spot in the area. Peaceful and beautiful, with an extraordinary art collection and a lovely garden patio. Reservations advised. Mon–Sat 6pm–10.30pm.

Rose Café and Market $–$$ *220 Rose Avenue, Venice, tel: 310-399 0711,* www.rosecafe.com. This casual café offers enticing bakery and deli fare plus various pizzas and inexpensive entrées. Mon–Fri 8am–3pm (counter 7am–5pm), Sat–Sun 8am–5pm.

Rustic Canyon $$$ *1119 Wilshire Boulevard, Santa Monica, tel: 310-393 7050,* www.rusticcanyonwinebar.com. This lovely and intimate wine bar and restaurant features a regularly changing menu of market-fresh dishes that use local and sustainable ingredients. Sun–Thu 5.30–10.30pm, Fri–Sat 5.30–11.30pm.

Valentino $$$–$$$$ *3115 Pico Boulevard, Santa Monica, tel: 310-829 4313,* www.valentinosantamonica.com. Expensive but worth every penny, this renowned Italian restaurant has an amazing wine list and top-notch food served in a formal dining room. Reservations recommended. Fri for lunch 11.30am–2.30pm, dinner Tue–Thu 5–10pm, Fri–Sat 5–10.30pm.

DOWNTOWN

Church & State Bistro $$–$$$ *1850 Industrial Street #100, tel: 213-405 1434,* www.churchandstatebistro.com. This lively and hip French bistro features nearly two dozen types of wine and reputedly one of the best raw bars in town. Lunch Mon–Fri 11.30am–2.30pm, dinner Mon–Thu 6–10pm, Fri 6–11pm, Sat 5.30–11pm, Sun 5.30–9pm.

Engine Company No. 28 $$–$$$ *644 South Figueroa, tel: 213-624 6996, www.engineco.com*. All-American food (firehouse chili, grilled fish and steaks, corn chowder, and lemon meringue pie) in an historic firehouse favored by lunching lawyers. Daily 11am–10pm.

The Palm $$$–$$$$ *1100 S. Flower Street tel: 213-763 4600, www. thepalm.com*. From the perfect steaks to the Nova Scotia lobsters flown in daily, the traditional American food is impeccable at this acclaimed Northern Italian steakhouse with New York origins. Lunch Mon–Fri 11.30am–3pm, dinner Mon–Thu 3–10pm, Fri 3–11pm, Sat 5–11pm, Sun 5–9.30pm.

Sushi Gen $$–$$$ *422 East Second Street, tel: 213-617 0552, www. sushigen-dtla.com*. The melt-in-your-mouth toro and salmon understandably attract crowds of people to this gem of a sushi restaurant in Little Tokyo. Go at lunch to beat the crowds and take advantage of the reasonably priced lunch specials. Lunch Mon–Fri 11.15am–2pm, dinner Mon–Fri 5.30–9.30pm, Sat 5–9.30pm.

Water Grill $$$–$$$$ *544 South Grand Avenue, tel: 213-891 0900, www.watergrill.com*. A stunning international seafood restaurant with a lively, upscale atmosphere and some of the best seafood Downtown. Lobster, crab, and oyster bar. Mon–Thu 11.30am–10pm, Fri 11.30am–11pm, Sat 5–11pm, Sun 4–10pm.

PASADENA

Dog Haus $ *105 N. Hill Avenue, tel: 626-577 4287, www.doghaus.com*. Excellent good-sized and generously built hot dogs and burgers with delicious toppings that will surely put a big smile on your face. This place is consistently busy and it can get really crowded at lunch time. Other locations in Los Angeles County. Daily 11am–10pm.

Parkway Grill $$$ *510 South Arroyo Parkway, tel: 626-795 1001, www.theparkwaygrill.com*. One of Pasadena's top restaurants, serving such eclectic California fare as fresh fish, black bean soup, and pizza in a two-level indoor garden setting. Lunch Mon–Fri 11.30am–2.30pm, dinner Mon–Thu 5.30–9.30pm, Fri–Sat 5.30–10.30pm, Sun 5–9.30pm.

THE VALLEY

Mistral $$–$$$ *13422 Ventura Boulevard, Sherman Oaks, tel: 818-981 6650, www.mistralrestaurant.net.* Straightforward, quality, and affordable French bistro fare is served in a warm and convivial atmosphere. Mon–Fri 11.30am–2.30pm, 5.30–10pm, Sat 5.30–10.30pm, Sun 5–9.30pm.

Wolfgang Puck Bistro $$ *1000 Universal City Plaza, #152 Universal City, tel: 818-985 9653, www.wolfgangpuck.com.* California pizzas, fresh pastas, and tasty salads designed by the master chef. Large outdoor patio. Sun–Thu 11am–9pm, Fri–Sat 11am–11pm.

LONG BEACH

Belmont Brewing Company $–$$ *25 Thirty-Ninth Place, tel: 562-433 3891, www.belmontbrewing.com.* Authentic brewery on the beach with a commanding view of the Long Beach skyline, Palos Verdes, and Catalina Island. Salads, sandwiches, pasta, meat, and fish entrées, and, of course, beer. Mon–Fri 11.30am–9.30pm, Sat 10am–10pm, Sun 10am–9.30pm; bar until midnight.

The Sky Room $$$–$$$$ *40 S. Locust Avenue, Long Beach, tel: 562-983 2703, www.theskyroom.com.* First opened in 1926, this classy restaurant atop the Breakers Hotel transports diners to an earlier era of fine dining, dancing, and entertainment, with stunning Art-Deco décor, California-French cuisine, romantic music, and panoramic views over the ocean and city. Extensive wine list. Reservations suggested. Mon–Thu 5.30–10pm, Fri–Sat 5.30pm–11pm, Sun 4.30–9pm.

ORANGE COUNTY

Crab Cooker $–$$ *2200 Newport Boulevard, Newport Beach, tel:*

949-673 0100, www.crabcooker.com. In this funky and fun dining room you'll get inexpensive mesquite-grilled fresh seafood. Sun–Thu 11am–9pm, Fri–Sat 11am–10pm.

Las Brisas $$$ *361 Cliff Drive, Laguna Beach, tel: 949-497 5434,* www.lasbrisaslagunabeach.com. Great Mexican cuisine, including seafood dishes, served on an outdoor patio or indoor dining room with marvelous views of the ocean. Mon–Thu 8am–10pm, Fri–Sat 8am–11pm, Sun 9am–10pm.

Medieval Times Dinner and Tournament $$$ *7662 Beach Boulevard, Buena Park, tel: 866-543 9637,* www.medievaltimes.com/buenapark. A wacky but original dinner-theater concept: you enjoy a fixed-price four-course meal (adults: $61.95; 12 and under $36.95) while watching knights on horseback and dueling sword fighters. Reservations advised. Dinner shows nightly, call castle for specific times; castle opens 90 minutes before showtime.

Steve's No. 4 Charbroil $ *6033 Warner Avenue, Huntington Beach, tel: 714-848 1422.* Steve's has been on the corner of Warner and Springdale for over 25 years, serving cheap breakfasts, great burgers and lunches. The family-run service is friendly and prices are very reasonable. Try the breakfast burrito but don't order a large fries unless you're ready to eat a lot. Daily 7am–9pm.

White House $$$ *887 South Anaheim Boulevard, Anaheim, tel: 714-772 1381,* www.anaheimwhitehouse.com. Award-winning northern Italian cuisine in a romantic mansion setting with log fires and elegant Victorian décor. Try the lobster ravioli or signature rack of lamb. Reservations required. Lunch Mon–Fri 11.30am–2pm, dinner nightly 5–10pm, brunch Sun 11am–3pm.

CATALINA ISLAND

Steve's Steakhouse $$$ *417 Crescent Avenue, Avalon, tel: 310-510 0333,* http://stevessteakhouse.com. Beautiful views over Avalon harbour and varied menu ranging from teriyaki chicken to surf n' turf. Daily lunch 11.30am–2pm, dinner 5–11pm.

A–Z TRAVEL TIPS

A Summary of Practical Information

A

ACCOMMODATIONS (See also Camping, Youth Hostels, and the list of Recommended Hotels starting on page 135)

Many top hotels offer special **promotional rates,** and winter travelers are likely to get a lower rate than during the summer tourist season, especially along the coast. It is always wise to have advance reservations: where available, use the toll-free 800, 844, 855, 866, 877 or 888 telephone numbers for making your reservations from within the US.

Hotel rates in Los Angeles are subject to a 15.57 percent tax, which is added on top of the quoted rates. Parking and telephone charges can add considerably to the bill. In addition, the better hotels have valet parking, which can cost from $6 to $40 or more per night; you are also expected to tip the valet at least $2 each time he delivers your car.

Beyond the hotel and motel options, self-catering **apartments** for longer stays (usually one-month minimum) are available. Oakwood Apartments (tel: 1-877 902 0832; www.oakwood.com) has properties in several locations throughout the city.

The Los Angeles Convention and Visitors Bureau (see page 131) publishes a **lodging guide,** as do most other information offices, listing a wide selection of accommodation options in and around the city.

AIRPORTS

Los Angeles International Airport (LAX) is one of the busiest airports worldwide, serving nearly 90 major airlines. It is located 17 miles (27km) from downtown LA, near the coast, off the 405 freeway. Planes arrive and depart from eight terminals and from the Tom Bradley International Terminal. The information number for LAX is 855-463 5252; www.lawa.org. Volunteer Information Professionals, who assist passengers with finding appropriate transportation or provide directions, can be found at information booths on the arrivals level of each LAX terminal.Frequent shuttle-bus service between terminals is provided free of charge. LAX shuttle buses are white with blue and green stripes. Board the 'A' shuttle under the LAX Shuttle sign. Fly Away buses provide cheap, 24-hour transport between Downtown and LAX (www.lawa.org/flyaway/default.aspx). There is also shuttle service to and from the Metro Rail Green Line Aviation Station. Plentiful taxis are also available.

Bob Hope Airport (BUR), formerly Burbank-Glendale-Pasadena Airport (tel: 818-840 8840; www.bobhopeairport.com) provides domestic services. It serves the San Fernando Valley as well as Los Angeles residents who prefer to avoid the chaos of LAX. Thirteen miles (20km) from downtown LA and less crowded than LAX, this airport is actually the better option for travelers arriving from other US cities and planning to stay in the valleys, Pasadena, Hollywood, or Downtown. (However, fewer shuttles and taxis frequent this airport, making ground transportation more problematic).

John Wayne (Orange County) Airport (tel: 949-252 5200; www. ocair.com), 16 miles (25km) from Anaheim, serves the Orange County region. Eight major domestic airlines fly here from around the country. Several airlines also serve the **Long Beach Airport** (tel: 562-570 2600; www.lgb.org).

B

BEACHES

Access to public beaches is free, but fees (between $5 and $10) are charged in parking lots (car parks). Pets, alcoholic beverages, and bonfires are prohibited. Lifeguards are on duty year-round during daylight hours. Always swim in front of an open lifeguard tower where possible and keep an eye out for warning signs.

For maps, guides, and further information about beaches, call the Marina del Rey Visitors' Information Center/Los Angeles County Beaches and Harbors Information Center at 310-305 9545 (www. visitmarinadelrey.com; 9am–5pm, recorded information 24 hours).

BUDGETING FOR YOUR TRIP

The prices below are approximate and vary with the establishment.

Airport transfer. To Downtown: taxi $45+, Super Shuttle $17.

Bicycle rental. $7–$9 per hour, $20–$32 per day.

Bus and Metro fares. $1.75 base fare, 50¢ transfers. Specials: $7 day-pass; $25 weekly pass.

Car rental. Depending on the company and the season, prices can vary greatly. Count on $35–$50 per day with unlimited mileage (taxes and collision damage waiver included), usually less expensive by the week and by waiving the collision damage waiver.

Entertainment. Movies $10–$14, concert/dance $20–$60, theater $20–$65, nightclubs $10–$20 cover charge.

Hotels (double occupancy, per night, 5.57 percent tax is not included). Expensive $210 and up; moderate $110–$210, budget under $110.

Meals and drinks. Breakfast $5–$15, lunch $7–$20, dinner $12–$20 and up, beer $3.50 and up, mixed drink $5–$12, wine $5–$15 per glass, soft drink $1–$2, coffee $2 and up.

Museums. Adults $5–$15, children, students, and seniors $4–$12.

Parking lots (car parks). $2–$6 per hour; many have a maximum $5–$6 charge; Downtown ramps and hotel parking $12–$30 per day.

Sales tax. A sales tax of 9 percent is added to most purchases and restaurant bills.

Theme parks. Adults $50–$80, children $20–$74 entrance per day.

Tours. Half-day city tours $30 and up.

C

CAMPING

In nearby state or national parks a daily fee is generally charged per campsite and per vehicle. Information on the Santa Monica Mountains and camping can be requested from the **National Park Service** (tel: 805-370 2300; www.nps.gov/samo) or the **State Park Service** (tel: 916-653 6995 or 800-777 0369; www.parks.ca.gov). State park camping information and reservations are available by calling 800-444 7275 or at www.reserveamerica.com. You can also contact the visitor information centers at Big Bear Lake and Lake Arrowhead and on Catalina Island (see page 131) for details of camping in these areas.

CAR RENTAL (See also Driving and Money)

Major car rental firms include Enterprise (tel: 800-261 7331; www.enterprise.com), Dollar (tel: 800-800 4000; www.dollar.com), Hertz (tel: 800-654 3131; www.hertz.com), and National (tel: 800-222 9058; www.nationalcar.com). Prices vary on an almost daily basis, and automobile-club and other discounts are often available. Look into special weekly/weekend rates.

Collision damage waiver adds considerably to the cost. It's best to learn whether your own automobile insurance or credit card offers full coverage for rental cars and, if so, waive the collision damage coverage. Also, rates that include unlimited mileage are advised.

To rent a car, you will need a valid driver's license plus an International Driving Permit if your own license is in a language other than English. Many agencies set a minimum age for car rental at 21, others at 25. A major credit card is required for car rental.

CLIMATE

Los Angeles enjoys a temperate climate with low humidity. Daytime temperatures average 80°F (26°C) June–October and 69°F (20°C) November–May. The rainy season is November–March, although rainfall is moderate and periodic, broken by sunny days. The heat of summer, usually tempered by sea breezes, is more intense in the valleys and further inland. Monthly average temperatures are as follows:

	J	F	M	A	M	J	J	A	S	O	N	D
°C	18	19	21	22	23	25	28	28	28	25	23	20
°F	65	66	69	71	74	77	83	83	82	77	73	68

CLOTHING

Bring comfortable, casual clothes and shoes. In January and February you might want to pack clothes suitable for rain. Formal restaurants may require a jacket and tie for men and dress clothes for women; otherwise, casual chic is fine. Bring a jacket or sweater.

CONSULATES

Many countries maintain consulates or have overseas representatives in Los Angeles. Official embassies are in Washington, D.C.

Australia: 2029 Century Park East; tel: 310-229 2300; http://los angeles.consulate.gov.au.

Canada: 550 South Hope Street, 9th Floor; tel: 213-346 2700; www.losangeles.gc.ca.

Japan: 350 South Grand Avenue, Suite 1700; tel: 213-617 6700; www.la.us.emb-japan.go.jp.

South Africa: 6300 Wilshire Boulevard, Suite 600; tel: 323-651 0902; www.dirco.gov.za/losangeles.

United Kingdom: 2029 Century Park East, Suite 1350; tel: 310-789 0031; www.gov.uk/government/world/usa.

CRIME AND SAFETY (See also Emergencies and Police)

Like all urban areas in the US, there is crime in LA, but as infamous as LA's criminal activity is, statistically it fares well when compared with other major cities. Visitors should take the usual precautions.

The all-purpose emergency telephone number is **911**. For non-emergencies, call the local police department. Find the number in the phone book or ask your concierge.

D

DRIVING (See also Car Rental)

To get around the city easily you will have to drive. Drive on the right; pass (overtake) on the left. Unless there's a sign to the contrary, you can turn right on a red signal, providing you make a complete stop and check for pedestrians and traffic. Drivers and all passengers must wear seat belts; children under 8 must be in a child's car seat secured in the back seat unless they are 4 feet 9 inches tall (148 cm). Rental car companies now offer child seats. Pedestrians have the right-of-way at crosswalks. It is an offense to pass a school bus in either direction on a two-lane road when it is taking on or discharging passengers. Strict drunk-driving laws are enforced, and anyone found driving under the influence of alcohol will be arrested.

Motorcycles. It is illegal anywhere in the state of California to ride a motorcycle without a helmet.

Pedestrians. Jaywalking (crossing in the middle of the street or against a traffic signal) is a serious offense and carries a heavy fine.

Highways. Divided highways are called freeways, and LA has the world's most extensive freeway system. They are generally the fastest way to cross town, but avoid them during rush hours (7–9.30am and 3.30–7pm), when they are clogged with traffic. For information on freeway or highway conditions, call 800-427 7623 or visit www.sigalert.com.

Freeways have multiple lanes, especially where one or more freeways intersect, but lanes are usually clearly marked with their destination. Some routes have car pool lanes, usually the far left lane. It will be marked with diamonds, and it means you must have two or more people in the car to use that lane. (Use it with only one person in the car and you'll be fined close to $400.) Before setting out, study your map and determine the exact route you intend to take. Freeways have both a number and a name, and sometimes there are two names depending on which part of the city you're in and which direction you're heading. The list below should help you.

Alternate routes. Like everywhere else in the world Los Angeles roads are subject to constant maintenance work. Call the **California Transportation Department** (CalTrans) at 916-445 7623 or 800-427 7623 for an up-to-date recording on the status of all California roads or check online at www.dot.ca.gov/roadsandtraffic.html. If you want to drive across town, the 10 freeway usually provides easy access from Santa Monica to Downtown.

Speed limits. If there are no posted speed limit signs, the maximum speed is 25mph (40km/h), and 55mph (90km/h) on the freeways. Outside city limits, the limit on Interstate highways is 65mph (100km/h) with several 70mph (112km/h) segments.

Parking. Los Angeles has an abundance of parking restrictions, which are posted along the street. Be sure you're parked legally and not in an area that requires a permit during specified times. Vehicles parked in violation of parking regulations are quickly ticketed

Freeway Number	Freeway Name
1	Pacific Coast Highway (PCH)
2	Glendale
5	Golden State/Santa Ana
10	Santa Monica/San Bernardino
22	Garden Grove
57	Orange
60	Pomona
90	Marina
91	Artesia/Riverside
101	Ventura/Hollywood
105	Century Freeway
110	Pasadena/Harbor
118	Simi Valley-San Fernando Valley
134	Ventura
170	Hollywood
210	Foothill
405	San Diego
605	San Gabriel River
710	Long Beach

and/or towed. A red line on the curb means no parking, a green line indicates parking for 20 minutes only, and a white line means passenger loading and unloading only. Have a supply of coins for parking meters, although some of the newer ones do take credit cards. LA's parking lots (car parks) may be expensive for short-term stays but are cheaper than fines.

Gas (petrol) stations. Most service stations stay open in the evening and on Sunday. Most are self-service. If you have a credit card you can generally pay at the pump. Otherwise, you will have to go inside and pay in advance before the pump will be activated; you get a refund if you overpay. There are several grades of gasoline (petrol): regular unleaded (the cheapest) will suffice for most rental cars.

Breakdowns, accidents, and insurance. The **American Automobile Association (AAA)** offers its assistance to members of affiliated organizations from abroad. It also provides travel information within the US. Check the phone directory for the branch nearest you. **AAA**'s Emergency Road Services number is 800-AAA-HELP.

If you have car trouble on the freeway, try to pull off the road to the right shoulder where there are emergency call boxes; get out on the passenger side away from traffic. If your car stalls in a traffic lane, turn on your emergency flashers and stay inside with your seat belt fastened while you wait for a passing patrol car. Never cross the freeway to reach a call box. Most accidents must be reported to the police at once. If one occurs, make sure you get the driver's license number and car license plate of all parties involved for your insurance claim.

E

ELECTRICITY

Throughout the United States the standard is 110 volts, 60 cycle AC. Plugs usually have two flat prongs. Overseas visitors without dual-voltage travel appliances will need a transformer and adapter plug.

EMERGENCIES (See also Medical Care and Police)
All-purpose emergency number: **911**

G

GAY AND LESBIAN TRAVELLERS
West Hollywood is the center of gay and lesbian life in LA. The magazine *Frontiers* (www.frontiersmedia.com) offers information on local LGBT events, arts, and entertainment. The annual LGBT Film Festival Outfest (www.outfest.org) is a popular event. For more information, you can also contact the Los Angeles LGBT Center (www.lalgbtcenter.org), the world's largest provider of LGBT services. The center has six branches in the city. In a historic moment, same-sex marriage was legalised throughout the US in June 2015.

GETTING THERE
By air from North America. Direct flights connect many American and Canadian cities to Los Angeles. Special fares are available on these competitive routes. Certain US airlines offer bargains for foreign travelers who visit several American destinations. Fly-drive vacations, including flight, hotel, and rental car, are offered by many airlines.

International flights. All the major international carriers have either direct or one-stop flights to Los Angeles from Europe and the main Pacific airports. Fares vary widely according to the season, but discounted fares to Los Angeles are usually available. There are various APEX fares if you book two to three weeks in advance and stay between seven days and six months.

By rail. Amtrak is America's passenger railway company. LA's Amtrak terminal is located Downtown at Union Station, 800 North Alameda Avenue. You can travel nationwide from here; coastal routes go north to Santa Barbara, Oakland, and Seattle and south to San Diego. For information call 1-800-872 7245; www.amtrak.

com. The Amtrak stations in Orange County are at Anaheim, Santa Ana, Fullerton, San Juan Capistrano, San Clemente, and Irvine.

By bus. The Greyhound bus terminal for long-distance coach travel is located Downtown at 1716 East Seventh Street. For additional terminal locations in the area, or for fare and schedule information, call 213-629 8401 or 1-800-231 2222; www.greyhound.com.

By car. The excellent Interstate freeway system criss-crosses the United States and links LA with all regions of the country.

GUIDES AND TOURS

Many tour companies are listed on the website run by the Los Angeles Convention and Visitors Bureau (www.discoverlosangeles. com; see page 131). Long-established firms include Starline Tours (323-463 3333; www.starlinetours.com), which take passengers past movie stars' homes; Dearly Departed Tours (tel: 855-600 3323; www. dearlydepartedtours.com), a tour of Hollywood's most infamous murders, deaths, and scandals. The Los Angeles Conservancy (tel: 213-623 2489; www.laconservancy.org) offers excellent walking tours of downtown LA. Details of self-guided walking tours of other areas can be obtained from tourist information offices (see page 131).

M

MEDIA

Radio, television and DVDs. Most hotel rooms have television and many have radio. Stations generally broadcast around the clock, and there are several foreign-language stations. The nationwide commercial networks are CBS, 4 ABC, 7 ABC, and Fox. Channel 28 (KCET) is a non-commercial educational, independent television channel. Many hotels also offer a range of cable-TV programs. Note that DVDs bought in the US will only work outside the US and Canada on 'Multi-Region' DVD players, so check yours first.

Newspapers and magazines. *The Los Angeles Times* (www.latimes.

com) is LA's main daily newspaper. The 'Calendar' section carries arts and entertainment listings; the Friday and Sunday editions are extensive. *Los Angeles Magazine* (www.lamag.com), published monthly, has interesting features about LA life and excellent restaurant and entertainment listings. A number of weekly and monthly publications are also good sources of information. They include the *LA Weekly* (www.laweekly.com), the best of the free weeklies for listings of what's on around town and the *Downtown News* (www.ladowntownnews.com).

Foreign-language newspapers. Foreign newspapers and magazines are sold at large newsstands, and at Book Soup bookstore (8818 Sunset Boulevard; tel: 310-659 3110; www.booksoup.com).

MEDICAL CARE (see also Emergencies)

No vaccinations are required or recommended by health authorities, unless you are arriving from an area with cholera or yellow fever.

Health care, especially hospitalization, is extremely expensive in the United States. Some hospitals might even refuse treatment without proof of insurance. Overseas visitors should therefore make arrangements before leaving home (through a travel agent or an insurance company) for **health insurance** with a high level of coverage.

If you do need **medical assistance**, contact any of the major hospitals. Most have 24-hour emergency (trauma) rooms. These include: St. John's Hospital and Health Center (2121 Santa Monica Boulevard; Santa Monica; tel: 310-829 5511); Cedars-Sinai Medical Center (8700 Beverly Boulevard; tel: 800-233 2771; http://cedars-sinai.edu); and Hollywood Presbyterian Medical Center (1300 North Vermont Avenue; tel: 213-413 3000; http://hollywoodpresbyterian.com/. For emergencies, dial 911.

Drugstores (pharmacies). Several drugstores stay open late or even 24 hours a day. You may find that some medicines obtainable over the counter at home are available only by prescription in the US, and vice versa. The large pharmacy chain Rite Aid (www.riteaid.com) has numerous locations throughout the LA area.

MONEY

Currency. The dollar ($) is divided into 100 cents (¢). **Banknotes**: $1, $2 (uncommon), $5, $10, $20, $50, and $100. Larger denominations are not in general circulation. All notes are the same size and the same green color, so be sure to double-check before you pay for something. **Coins**: 1¢ (known as a penny), 5¢ (nickel), 10¢ (dime), 25¢ (quarter), 50¢ (half dollar, less common). Dollar coins are rarely encountered.

Banks and currency exchange. Banks are generally open 9am–5 or 6pm Monday–Friday or Saturday. Other foreign-exchange outlets include **World Banknotes Exchange,** downtown at 520 S. Grand Avenue, Suite L100 (tel: 213-627 5404; www.wbxchange.com) and **Travelex**, 8901 Santa Monica Boulevard inside US Bank (tel: 310-659 6093; www.travelex.com).

Credit cards. Major credit cards are accepted in most hotels, shops, and restaurants. You may be asked for supplementary identification.

Money transfers. To find the nearest money transfer location, call **Western Union** at 800-325 6000; for Spanish speakers, call 800-325 4045; for money orders call 1-800-999 9660 (http://westernunion.com).

OPENING HOURS

Shops. Department stores and shopping malls are generally open 10am–9pm on weekdays, 10am–6 or 7pm on Saturday, and 11am–5 or 6pm on Sunday. Individual shops are generally open Monday–Saturday from 9 or 10am to 5.30 or 6pm. In trendy shopping areas such as Melrose Avenue, shops often stay open until 11pm.

Museums. Normally 10am–5pm, but many open longer at least one night a week or on Sunday. Most museums are closed on Monday or one other day of the week.

Banks. Generally Monday–Friday or Saturday 9am–5 or 6pm.

Post offices. Most branches open at 8.30 or 9am and close at 5pm, though some close later. Some are open on Saturdays, as well.

P

POLICE

Police wear dark blue uniforms and usually travel by car, motorcycle, or bicycle. In an emergency, dial **911**. The Los Angeles Police Department (LAPD) can be reached at 1-877-275 5273 or at www.lapdonline.org.

POST OFFICES

The US Postal Service deals only with mail. Check with your hotel concierge for the branch office nearest you. Post offices are generally open 8.30 or 9am–5pm Monday to Friday, and some are open 9am–3.30pm on Saturday. You can usually purchase stamps at the front desk in your hotel and at drugstores and grocery stores. Letters can be mailed from the hotel, or dropped in one of the blue mailboxes located throughout the city. For more information, call the Postal Answer Line toll free at 1-800-275 8777 or visit www.usps.com.

PUBLIC HOLIDAYS

When certain holidays (such as Christmas) fall on a Sunday, banks, post offices, and most stores close on the following Monday. They close on Friday if those holidays fall on a Saturday.

New Year's Day January 1
Martin Luther King Jr. Day Third Monday in January
Presidents' Day Third Monday in February
Memorial Day Last Monday in May
Independence Day July 4
Labor Day First Monday in September
Columbus Day Second Monday in October
Veterans' Day November 11

Thanksgiving Fourth Thursday in November
Christmas December 25

S

SMOKING

Smoking is banned in city restaurants and bars, although trendy spots have a tendency to ignore the rules. Laws vary in surrounding communities, but all restaurants are required to have a non-smoking section. Smoking is also prohibited in most public spaces.

T

TELEPHONES

The American telephone system is run by several private, regional companies. Coin- or credit card-operated phones are found in most public places, including hotel lobbies, drugstores, gas (petrol) stations, bars, restaurants, and along the streets. For directory assistance (information) dial **411**. When calling long-distance remember that evening (after 5pm) and weekend rates are often much cheaper.

The Greater Los Angeles area has four **area codes**: **310** (Westside, Beverly Hills, Santa Monica, and Los Angeles International Airport); **213** (Downtown LA); **323** (Hollywood); and **562** (Long Beach). Other area codes are **818** (San Fernando Valley), **626** (San Gabriel Valley and adjacent areas), **714** and **949** (Orange County), and **909** (Riverside and San Bernardino counties).

Callers dialing from one area code to another must always dial 1 plus the appropriate area code and seven-digit number. Local long-distance charges sometimes apply; these are based on a zone system and are difficult to work out in advance.

TELEVISION TICKETS

Tickets for most television show recordings on all networks are now handled by companies such as Audiences Unlimited (tel: 818-260 0041; www.tvtickets.com) or TVTix (tel: 818-985 8811; www.tvtix.com). Tickets can also be obtained in person on the day of the show. They are usually limited to two per person and are given on a first-come, first-served basis. All tickets are free and are offered online for most shows starting about 30 days prior to the show date. If you need to write in for tickets for specific shows, this information will come up on the website. TVTix also operates a second website, www.beinamovie.com, which can help you take part in a movie crowd scene. For *The Price is Right*, call 855 447 7423 or go to cbs.com for that and other CBS shows. Paramount Studios tickets are available through Audiences Unlimited, above.

TIME DIFFERENCES

Los Angeles is in the Pacific time zone, 8 hours behind GMT. From the second Sunday in March to the first Sunday in November, the clock is advanced 1 hour for Daylight Saving Time (GMT minus 7 hours). The chart below shows the time worldwide when it is noon in Los Angeles.

Los Angeles	Chicago	New York	London	Sydney	Cape Town
noon	2pm	3pm	8pm	6am	10pm

TIPPING

You should add 18 percent to restaurant and bar bills. If service has been very good, 20 percent or more is appropriate. Cinema/theater ushers are not tipped, but doormen who provide a service (calling a cab, etc) and cloakroom attendants should be given no less than one dollar. Tip the parking valet when he brings your car for you (not when he parks it). Some general guidelines:

Porter $1–$2 per bag
Hotel housekeeping $1–$2 per day except for one-night stays, or $7–$15 per week

Hotel concierge $5 for tickets or restaurant reservations ($10 or more if they're hard to get)
Taxi drivers about 15 percent
Tour guide 10–15 percent
Parking valet $2

TOURIST INFORMATION

The **Los Angeles Convention and Visitors Bureau** runs the site www.discoverlosangeles.com, which contains a visitors' guide to the city.
Visitor information centers. Most visitors' centers will gladly send you tourist information:

Hollywood Visitor Information Center, 6801 Hollywood Boulevard, at Hollywood and Highland, Hollywood, CA 90028; tel: 323-467 6412. Monday–Saturday 9am–10pm, Sunday 10am–7pm.

Union Station, 800 N. Alameda St. Port of Los Angeles, Berth 93, Pacific Cruise Ship Terminal, San Pedro, tel: 310-514 9484

Anaheim/Orange County Visitor and Convention Bureau, 800 West Katella Avenue, Anaheim, CA 92802; tel: 855-405 5020; http://visit anaheim.org.

Big Bear Lake Resort Association, 630 Bartlett Road, Big Bear Lake, CA 92315; tel: 800-424 4232; www.bigbearinfo.com.

Catalina Island Chamber of Commerce and Visitors Bureau, PO Box 217, Avalon, CA 90704; tel: 310-510 1520; www.catalinachamber.com.

Lake Arrowhead Communities Chamber of Commerce, 28200 California 189, Lake Arrowhead, CA 92352; tel: 909-336 1547; www.lake arrowhead.net.

Long Beach Area Convention and Visitors Bureau, 301 E. Ocean Boulevard, Suite 1900, Long Beach, CA 90802; tel: 562-436 3645 or 800-452 7829; www.visitlongbeach.com.

Palm Springs Desert Resorts Communities Convention and Visitors Authority, 70–100 Highway 111, Rancho Mirage, CA 92270; tel: 760-770 9000 or 1-800-967 3767; www.visitgreaterpalmsprings.com.

Pasadena Convention and Visitors Bureau, 300 E. Green Street,

Pasadena, CA 91101; tel: 626-795 9311 or 1-800-307 7977; www. visitpasadena.com.

TRANSPORTATION

Although Los Angeles has an extensive bus and now rail and subway network, use of a car is generally recommended because of the distance between sights and attractions and the travel time involved. But for short trips, or for carefree sightseeing at low cost, it's easy to ride the MTA, which is getting more comprehensive all the time.

Buses/rail transit. The Los Angeles County Metropolitan Transportation Authority (MTA) provides bus, light rail, and subway transportation in the metro area. Subway and light rail now connect Downtown with Hollywood, Universal City, Pasadena, and many tourist destinations. The Metro Orange Line serves the San Fernando Valley with new MetroLiner buses. The Expo Lines light rail system operates between Downtown Los Angeles and Culver City, with the lastest extension servicing Santa Monica. For information on MTA bus/rail/subway services and routes, call 323-GO METRO (226 6883), or consult the Trip Planner on its website, www.metro. net. Base fare is $1.75, plus 50¢ for transfers. You must have the exact fare or a token; drivers do not give change. A day pass, good on all Metro buses and rail lines, is $7; weekly passes are $25.

The Los Angeles Department of Transportation operates the DASH shuttle system (tel: 213-808 2273; www.ladottransit.com/ dash) Downtown during the daytime, linking the major business, civic, and entertainment centers (50¢ per ride; free transfer). It also runs the Commuter Express system. Separate DASH systems also operate around Hollywood and throughout the city. A similar shuttle system, the Passport, operates in Long Beach.

Taxis. There are taxi ranks at airports, train and bus terminals, and major hotels. Otherwise they are radio-dispatched and must be ordered by phone. Cabs will stop when hailed on the street, but they are infrequent.

Ferries. There are several services between the coast and Catalina Island. The Catalina Passenger Service operates the Catalina Flyer (tel: 949-673 5245; www.catalinainfo.com) once daily to and from Newport Beach: round-trip fares are $70 adults, $65 seniors (60+), $53 children 3–12, and $6 children under 2. Catalina Express (tel: 1-800-481 3470, 800-622 2354; www.catalinaexpress.com) offers several voyages a day from San Pedro, Long Beach, and Dana Point: round-trip fares are $74.50 adults, $68 seniors (55+), $59 children 2–11, $5 children under 2 (Dana Point departures slightly higher).

Bikes. A public bike-share system is scheduled to be launched in spring 2016 with 1,100 bikes at 65 stations in Downtown Los Angeles as a pilot project. Bikes will be available 24 hours a day and a smartphone app will provide information about their availability. Planned locations of dock stations include Union Station, the Convention Center, Staples Center, Grand Park, the Seventh Street Metro stop, Grand Central Market, Pershing Square, the Arts District and the future Figueroa Cycle Track (the city's first protected bike lane is located on Figueroa Street). In 2017, the bike-share scheme will be expanded to Pasadena. Eventually, 4,000 bicycles will be rolled out.

TRAVELERS WITH DISABILITIES

A number of properties have rooms for the disabled with handicapped-accessible features as well as wheelchair-accessible transportation and recreational facilities.

TDD telephone lines are available for the hearing impaired. Contact the California Relay Service for the Hearing Impaired: (Voice) 800-735 2922, (TDD/TTY) 800-735 2929.

Los Angeles County Metropolitan Transportation Authority's buses are equipped either with automatic wheelchair lifts, or, in the newer buses, low-floor access. The DASH system is similarly equipped. You can contact the Metro Wheelchair Lift Hotline (800-621 7828).

V

VISAS AND ENTRY REQUIREMENTS

Canadians need to present a valid passport, a NEXUS card, FAST-card or enhanced driver's license (EDL) as evidence of their nationality. See www.voyage.gc.ca for more information. Under the visa waiver program, UK, Irish, Australian, and New Zealand citizens do not need a visa for stays of less than 90 days in the US, only a valid 10-year passport and a return airline ticket. All passports must be machine readable, and visitors should check the current rules on biometric passports: www.travel.state.gov. The airline will issue a visa waiver form. Since September 11, 2001, new security arrangements have meant that non-American nationals are often called upon to produce photo ID. Plan to carry your passport with you at all times, or photocopy it and carry around the copies.

Duty-free allowances. You will be asked to complete a customs declaration form before you arrive in the US. When returning to your own country, restrictions will apply: depending on the country, usually around 200 cigarettes or 50 cigars or 250g tobacco, 2 liters wine or spirits.

Y

YOUTH HOSTELS

Hostels offer modest, low-cost alternative lodging – for all ages. Call for prices, restrictions, and reservations. The following hostels are in the Los Angeles area: Banana Bungalow (603 N Fairfax Avenue, West Hollywood, CA 90036; tel: 323- 655 2002; www.bananabungalow.com) is centrally located and provides low-cost tours and shuttles to major attractions. There is another location on Hollywood Boulevard. Hosteling International Los Angeles (1436 Second Street, Santa Monica, CA 90401; tel: 310-393 9913; www.hilosangeles.org) is the largest on the coast, located in the center of Santa Monica's beach action.

RECOMMENDED HOTELS

To make direct reservations with a hotel, we have included addresses (all in California, abbreviated CA) and telephone numbers and websites. Check-out time is generally 11am–12pm, with check-in usually available from 3pm to 4pm. All hotels accept major credit cards.

Rates vary greatly according to season and availability; many hotels offer special weekend packages, business rates, and promotions. Ask about such discounts when booking. We have used the following symbols to indicate room prices (two persons in a double room, per night):

$$$	over $210
$$	$110-$210
$	under $110

HOLLYWOOD

Best Western Plus Hollywood Hills Hotel $$ *6141 Franklin Avenue, Hollywood 90028, tel: 323-464 5181, toll-free 800-287 1700,* www.best western.com. Family-friendly, with a Hollywood theme. The guest rooms are divided into a newer motel-style building with a courtyard pool and an older building with large hotel-style rooms, many of which have kitchens. 86 rooms.

Chateau Marmont $$$ *8221 Sunset Boulevard, Hollywood 90046, tel: 323-656-1010,* www.chateaumarmont.com. Perched above the Sunset Strip, this is the discreet hideaway beloved of film stars and rock gods. If you're sitting in the bar, keep your *eyes* peeled to spot the celebrities. Choose between a suite, penthouse, garden cottage, or hillside or poolside bungalow.

Hollywood Roosevelt Hotel $$$ *7000 Hollywood Boulevard, Hollywood 90028, tel: 323-856 1970,* www.hollywoodroosevelt.com. Site of the first public Academy Awards, an historic hotel with classic, Spanish-revival décor and movie-star memorabilia. Courtyard, hot tub, pool, restaurant, cocktail lounge, and jazz club. 302 rooms and 80 suites.

MID-WILSHIRE

Beverly Laurel Motor Hotel $$–$$$ *8018 Beverly Boulevard, Los Angeles 90048, tel: 323-210 3076,* http://beverlylaurelmotorhotel. com. The basic motel-style rooms jazzed up with Art-Deco furnishings and colorful touches, as well as the cute courtyard pool, make this a favorite spot with young travelers in particular. Make sure to try out the adjoining hip late-night diner that serves good American-style food. 52 rooms.

The Orlando $$$ *8384 W. Third Street, Los Angeles 90048, tel: 323-658 6600, toll free 800-624 6835,* www.theorlando.com. Hip European-style boutique hotel with large rooms, a short walk from good restaurants and shopping areas, such as the Beverly Center, Third Street, and Farmers Market. Amenities include free internet access in public areas, saltwater swimming pool, fitness center, restaurant, lounge. 98 rooms.

WEST HOLLYWOOD

Mondrian Hotel $$$ *8440 Sunset Boulevard, West Hollywood CA 90069, tel: 323-650 8999, toll-free 800-606 6090,* www.mondrian hotel.com. This trendy, celebrity-frequented hotel plays on scale and illusion and exudes Hollywood attitude. Minimalist chic rooms usually come with kitchens and provide VIP access to the outdoor lounge, the SkyBar. 237 rooms and suites.

The Standard $$–$$$ *8300 Sunset Boulevard, West Hollywood 90069, tel: 323-650 9090,* www.standardhotel.com. One of the hippest hotels on the strip, with cool rooms, pool, workout room, vista terrace, restaurant, bar, and live DJ at the front desk. The lobby regularly features art videos and live performances. 138 rooms, 2 suites.

Sunset Tower Hotel $$$ *8358 Sunset Boulevard,West Hollywood 90069, tel: 323-654 7100,* www.sunsettowerhotel.com. Historic luxury hotel with landmark Art-Deco façade. Pool and terrace with city views, health center, sauna, library, restaurant, bar, and lounge. 74 rooms and suites.

Four Seasons at Beverly Hills $$$ *300 South Doheny Drive, Los Angeles 90048, tel: 310-273 2222, 310-786 222, www.fourseasons.com.* Refined luxury accommodations with excellent service and lots of celebrity-watching potential. Rooms are well appointed and have small balconies and beautiful bathrooms. Excellent fourth-floor pool and outdoor gym, a spa, concierge, restaurants, lively cocktail lounge. 285 rooms.

L'Ermitage Beverly Hills Hotel $$$ *9291 Burton Way, Beverly Hills 90210, tel: 310-278 3344, toll-free 877-235 7582, www.lermitagebh.com.* The highly-acclaimed ultra-luxury hotel is modern-minimalist and high-tech. The stylish lobby lounge and rooftop restaurant (with panoramic views), swimming pool, spa, gym, and sauna are second only to the accommodations, which start at 600 sq ft (56 sq m) and come with huge bathrooms, wet bars, four phone lines, personal fax machines, huge TVs, DVDs, and fancy stereo systems. 100 rooms, 19 suites.

The Regent Beverly Wilshire $$$ *9500 Wilshire Boulevard, Beverly Hills 90212, tel: 310-275 5200, www.fourseasons.com.* The elegant lobby of this historic hotel at the base of Rodeo Drive gives way to sumptuous rooms with plush furnishings and luxurious marble baths. Pool, fitness center, spa with steam room and sauna, restaurant, bar, shops. 395 rooms and suites.

Hyatt Regency Century Plaza $$$ *2025 Avenue of the Stars, Los Angeles 90067, tel: 310-228 1234, toll-free 888-591 1234, www.centuryplaza.hyatt.com.* Business hotel with spacious accommodations featuring marble baths and attractive furnishings. Landscaped garden, restaurant, cocktail lounge, pool, fitness center, spa with café, business center, shops. 726 rooms and suites.

Cal Mar Hotel Suites $$$ *220 California Avenue, Santa Monica 90403, tel: 310-395 5555, toll-free 800-776 6007, www.calmarhotel.com.*

Large apartment-style suites surrounding a courtyard pool – perfect for families. Coin laundry. A few blocks from Third Street Promenade and the beach. 36 suites.

Loews Santa Monica Beach Hotel $$$ *1700 Ocean Avenue, Santa Monica 90401, tel: 310-458 6700, toll-free 888-332 0160, www.loews hotels.com.* Casually luxurious beachfront hotel with a five-story glass atrium and outdoor swimming pool. Perched above the beach, two blocks from Santa Monica Pier. Some rooms have ocean views. Two restaurants, bar, pool, Jacuzzi, sundeck, fitness facility with steam and dry saunas; business center, bike and skate rental. 325 rooms, 17 suites.

Shangri-La Hotel $$$ *1301 Ocean Avenue, Santa Monica 90401, tel: 310-394 2791, toll-free 877-999 1301, www.shangrila-hotel.com.* Stylish Art-Deco design makes this 1939 beachside hotel near the Santa Monica Pier an architectural gem. In 2008 the hotel was completely refurbished with a contemporary twist, including such amenities as high-speed internet and sound systems, lavish suites, elevated pool and cabanas, chic rooftop bar and gourmet restaurant. 71 rooms and suites.

Shutters on the Beach $$$ *One Pico Boulevard, Santa Monica 90405, tel: 310-458 0030, www.shuttersonthebeach.com.* The only hotel in Santa Monica right on the beach. Exquisitely appointed rooms in luxury cottage-style setting. Public areas with fireplaces and original artwork. Two restaurants and bars, pool, Jacuzzi, sauna, health club, spa, and bicycle and skate rental. 186 rooms, 12 suites.

DOWNTOWN

Figueroa Hotel $ *939 S. Figueroa Street, Los Angeles 90015, tel: 213-627-8971, www.figueroahotel.com.* A onetime YWCA has been transformed, Hollywood-style, into an exotic, Moroccan-inspired reverie. Happily, it's also a bargain by LA standards. Rooms have wrought-iron beds and there's a pool out back for enjoying the California sun.

Hilton Checkers Hotel $$$ *535 South Grand Avenue, Los Angeles 90071, tel: 213-624 0000, toll-free 800-445 8667, www.hilton.com.* Historic and intimate deluxe boutique hotel. Rooms elegantly appointed with antiques and fine artwork. Gourmet restaurant and lobby bar, rooftop pool, and Jacuzzi. 188 rooms and suites.

Omni Los Angeles Hotel $$$ *251 South Olive Street, Los Angeles 90012, tel: 213-617 3300, toll-free 888-444 6664, www.omnilosangeles. com.* Downtown's cheeriest business hotel, next to MOCA, is brightened with artworks, while the spacious rooms are of contemporary design. Lounge, restaurant, executive floor, health club, pool, and saunas. 453 rooms and suites.

Westin Bonaventure Hotel $$$ *404 South Figueroa Street, Los Angeles 90071, tel: 213-624 1000, toll-free 800-353 1254, www.westin. com/bonaventure.* The busy atrium lobby gives way to shops, 17 restaurants, lounges, and numerous services. Glass elevators with spectacular city views transport guests to the revolving rooftop restaurant as well as the small but comfortable guest rooms. Outdoor pool, with floor-to-ceiling views, executive floor, spa, and health club. 1,354 rooms, 135 suites.

SAN FERNANDO VALLEY

Holiday Inn Burbank $$–$$$ *150 East Angeleno Avenue, Burbank 91502, tel: 818-841 4770, toll-free 800-311 1216, www.holiday-inn.com.* Towers with restaurant, pool, sauna, business facilities. 383 rooms, 102 suites.

Sheraton Universal $$–$$$ *333 Universal Hollywood Drive, Universal City 91608, tel: 818-980 1212, toll-free 800-325 3535, www.sheraton. com/universal.* Large, upscale rooms, some with sweeping views of the Hollywood Hills; five minutes from Universal Studios, Amphitheater, CityWalk. Pool, whirlpool, gym, restaurant, lobby bar, gift shop. 436 rooms and suites.

PASADENA

The Langham Huntington Hotel and Spa $$$ *1401 South Oak Knoll Avenue, Pasadena 91106, tel: 626-568 3900, www.pasadena.langham*

hotels.com. A stunning, historic pastoral resort that opened in 1907. Picture Bridge and Japanese gardens. Three restaurants, three lounges, pool, jacuzzi, executive floors, fitness center, and tennis courts. Afternoon tea available daily. 380 rooms, suites, and cottages.

LONG BEACH

Hotel Queen Mary $–$$ *1126 Queens Highway, Long Beach 90802, toll-free 877-342 0742, 877-342 0738, www.queenmary.com.* Formerly the world's largest passenger ship, this historic liner is now docked in the harbor and converted into a hotel. Several restaurants, bar, spa, and on-board shopping. Tours are available. 307 unique staterooms and suites.

Westin Long Beach $$–$$$ *333 East Ocean Boulevard, Long Beach 90802, tel: 562-436 3000, toll-free 800-937 8461, www.westin.com/long beach.* Offering spacious rooms with full bay-window and ocean views. Situated across from the Convention Center. Restaurant, lobby bar, pool, fitness center, saunas, business center. 469 rooms and suites.

ORANGE COUNTY

Anaheim Majestic Garden Hotel $$ *900 S. Disneyland Drive, Anaheim 92802, tel: 714-778 1700, toll-free 844-227 8535, www.majesticgarden hotel.com.* This hotel is fashioned after a medieval castle, with period décor, courtyards, and waterfalls. There's a Disneyland shuttle, and facilities include a restaurant, lounge, arcade, fitness center, and pool. 489 spacious rooms and suites.

Candy Cane Inn $$ *1747 South Harbor Boulevard, Anaheim 92802, tel: 714-774 5284, toll-free 800-345 7057, www.candycaneinn.net.* Budget-priced considering the amenities. Lovely, family-friendly motel with attractive landscaping, pool with children's wading area, Jacuzzi, free continental breakfast, and complimentary Disneyland shuttle. 171 rooms.

Disneyland Hotel $$$ *1150 Magic Way, Anaheim 92802, tel: 714-778 6600, www.disneyland.com.* Connected to the theme park by the monorail, this hotel extends the Disney formula with classic-Disney decorations, landscaped gardens, a marina with pedal boats, fantasy water show, and a variety of family activities. Numerous restaurants and lounges, three swimming pools, and entertainment. 990 rooms.

The Disney's Paradise Pier Hotel $$$ *1717 S. Disneyland Drive, Anaheim 92802, tel: 714-999 0990,* www.disneyland.com. Disney's more upscale hotel is adjacent to its sister property and honors the contemporary Disney characters. Restaurant and two bars, conference facilities, rooftop pools with a waterslide, and a fitness club. 489 rooms.

Newport Beach Marriott Hotel and Spa $$–$$$ *900 Newport Center Drive, Newport Beach 92660, tel: 949-640 4000, toll-free 866-440 3375,* www.marriott.com. Overlooks Newport Harbor yacht basin and the beach and ocean. Restaurant, lounge, lighted tennis courts, two pools, fitness center, and whirlpool. 512 rooms, 20 suites.

The Westin South Coast Plaza $$–$$$ *686 Anton Boulevard, Costa Mesa 92626, tel: 714-540 2500, toll-free 888-627 7213,* www.westin southcoastplaza.com. Comfortable, spacious rooms with luxury appointments. Central location for coastal and inland Orange County attractions. Adjacent to the Performing Arts Center and South Coast Plaza shopping center. The excellent restaurant offers indoor/outdoor seating. Cocktail lounge, pool, tennis courts, fitness center. 393 guest rooms.

CATALINA ISLAND

Hotel Metropole $$$ *205 Crescent Avenue, Avalon 90704, tel: 310-510 1884, toll-free 800-541 8528,* www.hotel-metropole.com. Situated on the beachfront in the Metropole Market Place. Some of the rooms with ocean views, fireplaces, spas, and private balconies. Restaurant, rooftop sundeck, and Jacuzzi. 48 spacious rooms and suites.

INDEX